RIOT!

OTHER BOOKS BY JULES ARCHER

African Firebrand: Kenyatta of Kenya
Angry Abolitionist: William Lloyd Garrison
Battlefield President: Dwight D. Eisenhower
Chou En-lai
Colossus of Europe: Metternich
Congo
The Dictators
The Executive "Success"
The Extremists: Gadflies of American Society
Famous Young Rebels
Fighting Journalist: Horace Greeley
Front-Line General: Douglas MacArthur
Hawks, Doves, and the Eagle
Ho Chi Minh: The Legend of Hanoi
Indian Foe, Indian Friend
Laws That Changed America
Man of Steel: Joseph Stalin
Mao Tse-tung: A Biography
Mexico and the United States
1968: Year of Crisis
Philippines' Fight for Freedom
The Plot to Seize the White House
Red Rebel: Tito of Yugoslavia
Resistance
Revolution in Our Time
Science Explorer: Roy Chapman Andrews
Strikes, Bombs, and Bullets: Big Bill Haywood and the I.W.W.
Thorn in Our Flesh: Castro's Cuba
They Made a Revolution: 1776
Treason in America: Disloyalty versus Dissent
Trotsky: World Revolutionary
Twentieth-century Caesar: Benito Mussolini
Uneasy Friendship: France and the United States
The Unpopular Ones
World Citizen: Woodrow Wilson

RIOT!

A History of Mob Action in the United States

Jules Archer

HAWTHORN BOOKS, INC.
Publishers/*New York*

RIOT!

Library of Congress Catalog Card Number: 74-6666

ISBN: 0-8015-5100-5

1 2 3 4 5 6 7 8 9 10

To
Lorraine and Bill Hutchings,
our charming good neighbors
for over a quarter of a century

Contents

1

Riots in Our Time

MONTGOMERY, Ala., May 20, 1961—"Here they come!" screams a brunette in a yellow dress. "Get those niggers!"

A mob of thousands besieges the Greyhound bus terminal wielding metal pipes, baseball bats, and other weapons. It surges toward an incoming bus carrying nineteen black and white college students—"Freedom Riders" determined to challenge illegal segregation in interstate bus travel.

Local police have been notified in advance with a request for protection. But when the bus door swings open, not one officer is in view. NBC-TV and Life photographers begin recording the arrival at the terminal.

*"Smash those **** cameras!"* Rioters hurl themselves at the cameramen, smashing their equipment on the ground. Students who try to enter the terminal are seized and thrown over a rail to a cement parking lot ten feet below the station. Their bags are flung after them, many bursting open.

Freedom Riders who are able to get up seek to flee the mob's fury. But they are pursued and clubbed, punched, or thrown to the ground. John Seigenthaler, an administrative assistant to Attorney General Robert F. Kennedy sent along as an observer, is knocked unconscious. Twenty-two of the Freedom Riders are injured.

Police arrive when the riot has raged for over twenty minutes. Making no effort to render first aid to the injured, they call for ambulances, which fail to show up. Asked why, Montgomery Public Safety Commissioner L. B. Sullivan replies, "It was broken down and could not come."

Gov. John Patterson assigns the blame for the riot at the bus terminal to the Freedom Riders. "I have no use," he says, "for these agitators or their kind."

OXFORD, Miss., September 30, 1962—As darkness falls a homemade fire bomb hurtles out of the mob gathered on the campus of the University of Mississippi. Its target is a black applicant being escorted to the administration building by two hundred federal marshals who are forced to run a gauntlet of spit and insults. The fire bomb hits a marshal's arm and fails to explode, but another one crashes against an army truck and sends it up in flames.

The throng of thousands has rallied in response to retired Gen. Edwin A. Walker's impassioned plea for ten thousand Southerners to flock to "Ole Miss" and help white students prevent the admission of James Meredith as the university's first black student on order of the Supreme Court.

A two-foot length of pipe whistles through the air, striking a marshal's helmet. Another marshal is hit by an uncapped bottle of acid and badly burned. The marshals drive back the excited hordes with cartridges of tear gas.

A newsman turns up his car radio loud as President John F. Kennedy begins broadcasting an appeal to white students at Oxford: "The eyes of the nation and all the world are upon you and upon all of us. And the honor of your university—and state—are in the balance. . . ."

Enraged rioters stone the car, smashing its windows.

Shots ring out, driving the marshals to cover. When two hundred national guardsmen rush on campus, they meet a hail of bricks and fire bombs. A brick breaks their commander's arm. Snipers fire at guardsmen's jeeps, wounding thirteen men. The mob sets five faculty cars ablaze in the main campus roads to block the arrival of federal troops speeding to the scene.

But soldiers soon storm on campus with loaded rifles and fixed bayonets, each fifth man armed with a riot shotgun. The mob attacks them with volleys of bricks, rocks, and fire bombs. Advancing through curtains of gasoline flames, the troops drive off the rioters. When the fifteen-hour siege is finally over, two men are dead, over seventy wounded.

But the mob has had the satisfaction of showing how it feels about letting an American citizen named James Meredith seek an education at the University of Mississippi.

WATTS DISTRICT, LOS ANGELES, August 12, 1965—All day long an angry rumor flashes around this 98 percent black ghetto like summer heat lightning. Police are reputed to have beaten up a black motorist for a traffic violation, clubbing down a pregnant black woman who protested. No one doubts the gossip; for years white police have been accused of using deliberate brutality to spread fear in the Watts ghetto, as a technique of control.

At twenty minutes after midnight an angry mob of seventy-five black youths begins hurling bricks at passing cars with white motorists. They are driven off by squad cars with wailing sirens and flashing red lights, but return as soon as the police leave and set five cars ablaze.

All next day the mood of Watts is sullen. A crowd of four hundred gathers in the street; trouble is in the air.

"Whitey's no good," one man shouts. "He talks about law and order. It's *his* law and *his* order—not *mine!*"

Other speakers work up mob passions by articulating bitter black complaints against being forced on welfare rolls to survive; against fourth-rate education in rundown schools; against being charged higher prices in the ghetto for food, clothes, and liquor than in white sections of Los Angeles; against the grinding poverty, sickness, vice, and crime in which blacks are forced to live; against police harassment and brutal treatment of black motorists; against 60 percent of all arrests in the city being made in Watts, which has less than 15 percent of the Los Angeles population.

Violence erupts again after midnight. This time mobs are led by "war counselors"—youths who communicate with each other through public telephone booths. Their attacks are directed principally against white property in the ghetto. Black shopowners hastily soap "Blood Brother" or "Soul Brother" on their windows, and their stores are spared.

Throngs surge through the streets overturning cars and setting them afire. Business buildings are burned until two whole blocks are blazing. Excited rioters yell hysterically, "Burn, baby, burn!" Firemen and any whites who enter the ghetto are driven off by sniper fire and hurled rocks and bottles. Looters break into white-owned stores, running out with arms full of clothing and merchandise.

Riot police form a skirmish line and fire warning shots over rioters' heads. Many racing looters refuse to halt when ordered, and some are shot down in flight. When sniper fire is reported from a tenement, police break in and rout its residents with blazing guns.

"You shot right into a houseful of babies," one woman accuses them. "Just because I'm a Negro doesn't mean I don't love my babies just as much as you love your white ones!"

The riot rages on for six days, with up to 10,000 people joining the tumultuous mobs. When the flames die down in Watts, 34 people are dead—28 blacks, 3 Mexican-Americans, 1 Japanese, and 2 policemen. Injured: 875. Arrested: nearly 4,000. The destruction of 209 buildings and the damaging of 789 more, in what is now grimly called "Charcoal Alley," is estimated at $200 million. Whole blocks lie in rubble and ashes. Hungry ghetto residents queue up in breadlines at makeshift relief stations, as helmeted troops patrol the wrecked streets with loaded weapons.

"Neither old wrongs nor new fears," President Lyndon B. Johnson angrily excoriates the mob, "can ever justify arson or murder. . . . A rioter with a Molotov cocktail [fire bomb] in his hands is not fighting for civil rights any more than a Klansman with a sheet on his back and a mask on his face. They are both . . . lawbreakers."

Indignation over police brutality is recognized as the spark that touched off the riot in Watts, but the tinder that fed the flames is a 30 percent unemployment rate. Watts is filled with unskilled migrants who have come to California vainly seeking jobs on the $2 billion annual payroll of Southern California's aerospace industries.

Embittered by watching TV programs showing white Americans living the good life while they are bottled up in poverty in the most densely packed ghetto in the country, the idle jobless of Watts have exploded in seething resentment.

The whites of Los Angeles are stunned and frightened. Gun sales soar by 1,000 percent in a single month. One week after the riot, police attack and demolish a Black Muslim mosque near Watts in a search for illegal weapons. Almost twenty thousand letters congratulate the chief of police.

Dangerous racial polarization threatens new outbreaks of violence in the cities of the nation.

OAKLAND, October 4, 1967—To climax a week of demonstrations against the controversial Vietnam War, San Francisco Bay Area dissenters and Berkeley student radicals escalate their protest to active resistance. Seeking to disrupt draft operations, four thousand demonstrators mill around the Oakland induction center, blocking its entrance.

Several hundred police charge the demonstration in a flying wedge. Wielding billy clubs and the disabling chemical spray, Mace, they knock down and trample dissenters underfoot, beating many of them unconscious in a ten-minute rampage.

ABC-TV cameraman Ralph Mayher is knocked down, kicked, his protective helmet torn off, and clubbed. He cries, "They're trying to kill me!" TV newscaster Jerry Jensen is sprayed in the eyes with Mace "by a cop who knew damn well I wasn't a demonstrator." UPI photographer Paul Gorman is knocked to the sidewalk by cops flailing nightsticks.

"I was on the ground and they hit me several times with nightsticks," he reports later. "They also kicked me in the head. I kept hollering I was with the press, but they didn't listen."

Oakland *Tribune* reporter Doug Eaton is hit across the eyes with a nightstick that shatters his glasses. Another *Tribune* reporter, Dick Spencer, is clubbed to his knees. AP cameramen Ernest Bennett and Robert Klein are also beaten.

Police violence sends twenty-four demonstrators and newsmen to the hospital; only one policeman requires medical treatment. When the demonstration is broken up, and the area cleared, buses unload draft inductees bound for Vietnam.

The president of the News Directors Association, Don Brice, accuses the police of being the real mob. "These attacks were not only unprovoked," he charges, "but it appeared to reporters on the scene that some members of the Oakland Police Department were deliberately selecting news people as targets for this treatment."

Gov. Ronald Reagan replies, "The work of the Oakland Police Department . . . was in the finest tradition of California's law enforcement agencies. The officers displayed exceptional ability and great professional skill."

He adds, "The taking of alleged grievances to the streets cannot and will not be tolerated."

WASHINGTON, D.C., April 4, 1968—When a white sniper assassinates Rev. Martin Luther King, the nation's foremost black leader, in Memphis, ghettos all over the United States erupt in outraged riots. Minutes after the broadcast news of King's death, stunned crowds gather in the streets on the edge of the capital's sprawling ghetto.

Black Power advocate Stokely Carmichael feeds their shock and rage. "Go home and get your guns," he cries. "When the white man comes he is coming to kill you. I don't want any black blood in the street. Go home and get you a gun and then come back, because I got *me* a gun!" He brandishes a pistol.

Roving bands of black teen-agers descend on Washington's downtown shopping district. Vengeful fires begin lighting the night sky. The small capital police force goes on alert as arson is followed by break-ins and looting.

The turmoil persists throughout the dawn, increasing all next day as looters dash in and out of shattered shop windows, carrying off booty in plain sight of the police.

"Take everything you need, baby!" one cries out to onlookers. An arrested looter protests, "They killed my brother—they killed Martin Luther King!" The officer demands wryly, "Was he stealing shoes when they killed him?"

Over seventy fires are burning and water pressure runs low as firemen desperately battle the conflagration to keep Washington from being razed. The fires and rioting spread dangerously close to the White House.

Forced to declare the capital endangered by "violence and disorder," President Johnson orders out sixty-five hundred army and National Guard troops. Helmeted combat forces guard the White House, bayoneted rifles at the ready. A machine-gun post defends the steps of the Capitol. The mobs are gradually brought under control, leaving behind them over $13 million worth of damage. A dusk-to-dawn curfew is imposed on the capital.

"I remember the sick feeling that came over me . . . as I saw the black smoke from burning buildings fill the sky over Washington," the president recalls later, "and as I watched armed troops patrolling the streets of the nation's capital for the first time since the Civil War, I wondered, as every American must have wondered, what we were coming to."

CHICAGO, August 28, 1968—All week long appalling scenes have swirled across the nation's TV newscasts, show-

ing helmeted cops clubbing teen-agers on bloodied pavements, and national guardsmen in gas masks spraying tear
gas at choking antiwar demonstrators at the Democratic
National Convention.

For the most part the demonstrators have been nonviolent but strident, shouting insults at the Chicago police.
When rushed, beaten, and scattered, some demonstrators
have hurled bottles, stones, shoes, and eggs at their uniformed assailants. Now, on the eve of nomination, crowds
begin surging toward convention headquarters, the Conrad
Hilton Hotel.

A shouting throng of five thousand gathers in Grant Park
across Michigan Avenue. Opposing President Johnson's
escalation of the Vietnam War, they demonstrate noisily
against the nomination of Vice-President Hubert Hum-
phrey, who supports that policy. The Chicago police are
enraged at the demonstrators, less by their political views
than by their taunts.

Many officers overreact with disproportionate force,
taking conspicuous pleasure in beating up long-haired
youths. Time and again they also attack reporters and
photographers, seeking to prevent any record being made
of police brutality. Clashes between police and demon-
stators create such turmoil that the National Guard is called
in to preserve order.

On nomination night tempers have reached flash point.
The police repeatedly wade into the crowds, swinging
nightsticks furiously and clubbing everyone in their path—
spectators, ministers, and newsmen as well as demonstrators.

Demonstrators seeking to press toward the hotel are
driven off by tear gas hurled by guardsmen with fixed
bayonets. Ordered to leave the area, thousands sit down
where they are, chanting, "Hell, no, we won't go!"—the
antiwar slogan.

11

The police charge wildly into the sit-downers, clubbing those on the ground as well as those who try to flee. Weeping people hurt in the crush cry for help. Police knock down people left and right, kicking them as they crumple. Girls who try to shield fallen boy friends are beaten and booted to tear them loose. Arrested demonstrators are dragged along the ground and hit with nightsticks.

A medic wearing a white coat and Red Cross armband is grabbed and beaten to the ground, his face bloody.

Part of the crowd is now trapped in front of the Hilton, pressed hard against a big plate glass window. The police thrust these people back violently, sending them crashing through the window. Bursting after them through the jagged glass, police begin clubbing everyone in the lobby who looks like a demonstrator.

A small number of enraged demonstrators respond with violence of their own, throwing firecrackers and blazing trash bins at the police. Some hurl rocks while others throw the sawhorses set up to block traffic. From a few upper-story windows of the Hilton, ashtrays, bricks, and other debris are thrown into the ranks of charging police.

A well-dressed woman indignantly protests the unnecessary brutality used in arresting demonstrators. An officer sprays Mace in her face and clubs her to the ground. He and two other policemen drag her by her arms to a paddy wagon, then throw her in bodily. Nearby, police on motorcycles charge into the crowd, knocking people down and running over them. Some victims are children ten to twelve years old.

Furious protests by many important Democratic leaders at the convention compel the withdrawal of all police from the area shortly after midnight.

The task of controlling the turbulence is turned over to the National Guard. The violence rapidly subsides, but by this time the "Battle of Chicago" has cost over 700 civilian and 83 police injuries, with 653 persons jailed. Miraculously, no one has been killed. Out of 300 newsmen assigned to cover the streets and parks of Chicago, the uncontrolled rage of the police has involved 65 in incidents resulting in injury to their persons or equipment, or their arrest.

Newsmen agree that while the police have had some provocation, their rampage has been an irresponsible overreaction. Acting as judge and jury, they have meted out street punishment to whole crowds, instead of making nonviolent arrests of specific offenders for a court of law to try.

The final verdict on the 1968 disorder · in Chicago is pronounced by President Johnson's own official National Commission on the Causes and Prevention of Violence. Its Walker Report, named after the commission's director, sums up its findings succinctly by describing the confrontation bluntly as a "Chicago police riot."

"There was no need for police violence at Chicago," observes Attorney General Ramsey Clark. "It did not maintain order, enforce law, prevent crime, or protect lives and property. It did the opposite."

Ironically, public opinion polls show that instead of criticizing the Chicago police, the majority of Americans are indignant at the TV networks for broadcasting news films revealing their brutality. Despite the testimony of their own eyes, they prefer to blame the riot on the demonstrators who were attacked and beaten on the streets of Chicago.

America's despairing young dissenters see this stubborn bias as one more example of the adult hypocrisy they consider responsible for the "generation gap" of the sixties.

KENT, Ohio, May 4, 1970—There are angry demonstrations on campuses across the country when President Richard M. Nixon expands the war in Vietnam by invading Cambodia. Students see his decision as a betrayal of his

13

campaign promise to bring the war in Southeast Asia to an end. They are further inflamed by the president's remark contrasting militant antiwar demonstrators—whom he labels "campus bums"—with young servicemen fighting in Vietnam.

At Kent State University a furious mob of four hundred students builds a protest bonfire in the town of Kent, then begins smashing the windows of various businesses to express their resentment of "the Establishment." Mayor Leroy Satrom proclaims a state of civil emergency and asks for national guardsmen, who are dispatched by Ohio Governor James Rhodes.

In retaliation, one or more student radicals burn down the ROTC building on campus. The guardsmen move onto the campus with loaded rifles and occupy it. At noon over twelve hundred students gather on the commons to protest both the invasion of Cambodia and the presence of the guardsmen. Ordered to disperse, students jeer, "Pigs off campus!"

The guardsmen fire tear gas from grenade launchers, forcing the students back. Almost a hundred helmeted, gas-masked guardsmen are ordered to advance with loaded weapons and fixed bayonets. From a distance a few students shout taunts and hurl rocks ineffectively at the advancing line.

In a scene eerily reminiscent of the Boston Massacre, the guardsmen suddenly open fire without order or warning. Fifteen students are hit and fall. Four—two boys and two girls—are killed. None of the four have been participating in the demonstrations, but have simply been watching or passing between classes. One girl slips to her knees beside a dead boy's sprawled body and screams in terror.

Student art major Lucia Perry, eighteen, later recalls, "I saw the men firing, and I saw the kids fall, and I looked out at the crowd and there were people . . . with blood all over them down the hill, and I just couldn't believe it. I've never seen people so mad and so horrified. . . . There's no way to describe the pain that I saw in people's faces."

Within a few days 450 colleges and universities shut down in protest against both the Kent State killings and the Cambodian invasion. One week later a nationwide student strike closes 2,500 institutions of higher learning—the first sustained national student strike in United States history.

The riot sparks an angry national debate. Who were the rioters—the demonstrators or the National Guard? A conservative county grand jury exonerates the guardsmen who killed the students, on grounds that the troops' lives had been endangered. The grand jury indicts instead students and faculty members involved in the demonstration.

Attorney General John Mitchell refuses to convene a federal grand jury, insisting that he has no evidence to indicate the need for an FBI investigation. But Sen. Stephen M. Young of Ohio brands the guardsmen "trigger-happy" and insists that the four students were brutally murdered.

An investigation by reporters of the Knight newspaper chain reveals that the four victims had not been involved in the demonstrations in any way; that the guardsmen had lied when they claimed to have been fired upon by a sniper; that some guardsmen had aimed deliberately at students, while others had fired in panic; and that none had been in danger.

Three years later a new attorney general, Elliot Richardson, agrees that the Ohio county grand jury hearings had been a whitewash of the guardsmen. Those who shot at the students are now indicted. One guardsman involved reveals, "The guys have been saying that we got to get together and stick to the same story, that it was our lives or them, a matter of survival. I told them I would tell the truth."

And the truth, he explains, is that the four students had

15

been killed by mob psychology in the guardsmen's ranks: "It was an automatic thing. Everybody shot, so I shot. I didn't think about it. I just fired. . . ."

The record shows that in just one five-year period, from 1963 to 1968, American mobs have killed two hundred people and seriously injured nine thousand more.

Why?

2

What Turns Individuals into Mobs?

A MOB, ACCORDING to the Oxford Dictionary, is "the lower orders; rabble, tumultuous crowd; promiscuous assemblage of persons." It stems from the Latin *mobile vulgus*, meaning an easily moved common herd or excitable crowd. Once a purely slang term, it is now standard English.

There is a distinction between a crowd and a mob. "To be a mob," observes etymologist Bergen Evans, "the crowd must be excited, disorderly and dangerous."

A mob may be inspired by idealistic aspirations for freedom, as were the mobs of the French, American, and Russian revolutionary periods. But it may also reflect the baser passions of human nature, like the lynch mobs of the Old West and South, and the anti-Catholic mobs who attacked American churches and convents in the 1830s. Essentially, the mob represents an out-of-control mass of individuals united by passions that drive them to simultaneous acts of violence.

Its excitement is expressed in four principal ways—surging mass movement, physical assaults upon other people, attacks upon property, and widespread looting. A riot often involves all four.

There are basically six types of mobs. Unled mobs react in panic or hysteria, like the mobs that stormed banks over rumors of bank failures in the days before deposit insurance. Punitive mobs organize against unpopular minorities, like those that persecuted the early Mormons for practicing polygamy.

Territorial mobs defend their "turf," like ghetto mobs that attack police or members of another minority group who invade their neighborhoods. Lynch mobs spread terror among detested groups and force them into submissive behavior, like the Ku Klux Klan in the Reconstruction South.

Vigilante mobs take the law into their own hands, like those in the Old West that formed "necktie parties" to execute cattle rustlers and horse thieves. Finally, law enforcement agents may themselves become lawless mobs when they riot out of control, like the Chicago police at the Democratic National Convention in 1968.

The public often confuses demonstrations with mob actions. Groups with special grievances have every legal right to organize mass demonstrations to advertise and press for their demands, as guaranteed by the First Amendment, as long as they do not initiate violence or break any laws. Such demonstrators are not a mob. They may *become* a mob, however, if some of them commit acts of violence, or if they are goaded into fighting by the attacks of police or hostile spectators.

A distinction should also be made between mob riots and revolutionary uprisings. Insurrection is *planned* rioting that occurs when grievances of a segment of society are ignored over a long period of time, causing despairing radicals to plot a total revolt against civil authorities and the system. Sometimes they wait until discontent provokes a spontaneous riot, then fan it to the magnitude of full-scale rebellion.

Americans have generally assumed that those who make up rioting mobs represent only a tiny fraction of their racial, religious, political, or economic groups. Conspicuous are a riffraff fringe of ne'er-do-wells, juvenile delinquents, idlers, troublemakers, and criminal types. President Johnson attributed the ghetto uprisings of the 1960s to a few "mean and willful men."

Gov. George Wallace of Alabama charged that riots of the decade were the work of a small conspiracy of Communist agitators bent upon destroying American society.

The "riffraff" theory is popular because it reassures the majority of Americans that there is no serious flaw in their society, since the rioting reflects only the dissatisfaction of a tiny minority. If only riffraff are involved, then all that is necessary to prevent future riots is to muzzle them forcefully and ban outside agitators. That eliminates any need to face serious social problems that may be at the bottom of the disturbances and that would take painful change and readjustment by the majority to correct.

But the National Advisory Commission on Civil Disorders (Kerner Commission) found "no evidence that all or any of the disorders . . . were planned or directed by any organization or group, international, national or local." It found further that the typical rioter was *not* a member of the criminal, unemployed, or migrant "underclass."

Like the tip of an iceberg, the mob often reflects a much larger mass resistance hidden from view. The Governor's Commission on the Los Angeles Riots reported in 1966 that while most blacks in the city did not themselves participate in the Watts riot, most nevertheless supported the rioters.

Most riots are spontaneous, touched off the way a dropped match ignites tinder into a mass of flame. The spark is invariably an incident or rumor; the tinder an accumulation of grievances by one group of the population against another.

Sometimes the rumor is all or partly true, but as often as not it is highly exaggerated. In a Harlem riot during World War II, a black soldier on leave tried to prevent a white policeman from arresting a black woman for disorderly conduct. In the fight both men ended up in the hospital, the policeman with head bruises, the serviceman with a bullet in his shoulder. The spark that provoked a riot was the rumor flashing through the black community that a white cop had shot a black soldier in the back and killed him, in the horrified presence of his mother.

Many mobs take the form of vigilante groups to avenge reported crimes against some of their number. Often the alleged crimes are murder, rape, physical assault, and theft, but just as often the offenses are merely social transgressions. Thus in 1856 the San Francisco vigilante committee organized mobs against all those it considered infringing its social code—Catholics, Jews, immigrants, blacks, labor leaders, radicals, and other such "undesirables."

A 1933 study of southern lynching found that at least a third of the victims lynched by mobs for alleged misdeeds had been falsely accused, and over half the lynchings had been carried out with police officers participating.

"The meaning of these facts," observed Swedish sociologist Gunnar Myrdal, "is that, in principle, a lynching is not merely a punishment against an individual but a disciplinary device against the Negro group." Lynchings were often sparked by as little provocation as a black's daring to testify in court against a white man, or his use of defiant language.

Racial riots in the North are fueled by a different tinder.

"Riots are most likely to occur," notes Algernon D. Black, former chairman of the New York Civilian Complaint

Review Board, "when new groups immigrate and when their effort to enter the housing market, the job market, and the schools becomes a threat to those who feel that the community is theirs."

Once the mob flames into action, the riot feeds on the larger fuel beneath the tinder—deep-rooted cultural prejudices. In ghetto riots a black mob's rage is fueled by centuries of slavery, oppression, and discrimination at the hands of white men. In antidraft riots a radical mob's rage is fueled by years of vain protest against war policies that profit corporations and compel youths to kill and be killed in wars of intervention. In riots against civil rights, a white mob's rage is fueled by bitter resentment at working hard to pay high taxes, some of which is spent as welfare aid to unemployed ghetto residents.

"Most groups which have engaged in mass violence," observes Richard E. Rubenstein, consultant to the Kerner Commission, "have done so only after a long period of fruitless, relatively nonviolent struggle in which established procedures have been tried and found wanting."

Angry mobs grow out of dissatisfied minorities when official promises of reform are not followed by action. A gap widens between expectations and fulfillment. In the 1950s and 1960s American blacks were promised speedy remedial action to give them equal opportunities in jobs, housing, and schools. But most found themselves continuing to live in the same intolerable conditions of grinding poverty, while "tokenism" permitted a few to escape the ghettos.

Frustration was the tinder that caught fire in nationwide urban risings. Part of that frustration was resentment of white patrols in the black community. Blacks saw them not as protectors but as guards confining them in the ghettos to keep them out of surrounding white communities. This belief was reinforced when police instantly sealed off the ghettos at the outbreak of a riot. Ghetto residents felt that police looked upon them not as individuals, but as faceless blacks who were to be dealt with harshly to "keep them in line."

Student revolts in the 1960s and early 1970s followed five years of promises by the government of an early end to the Vietnam War, only to have that war dragged on and on through the whole first Nixon administration.

Mobs are most likely to take matters into their own hands when a group finds that any protest against injustice is useless because "nobody's listening," or when the group's leaders are either too ineffective or too meek to command respectful attention from the minorities.

Americans who tolerate no excuse for disturbing law and order tend to forget that violent protest is part of our tradition as an instrument of last resort, when other avenues to just goals are shut off. This was the heritage of the American Revolution itself. A riot represents a convulsive seizure of society—a grave symptom of something desperately wrong that must be quickly examined and remedied.

The largest number of riots in America yesterday and today have had their roots in racial, religious, or ethnic hostilities, even when a riot has seemed to be about other issues. Thus election-day riots have often stemmed from a mob's effort to keep a minority group from voting. Labor riots have often reflected the determination of white workers to keep blacks, Orientals, Mexican-Americans, Puerto Ricans, or other ethnic groups out of their unions, factories, and communities.

There are few minority groups in the United States that have not felt the wrath of mobs at one time or another.

"Almost all immigrant groups went through a period of unpopularity," observes sociologist Allen D. Grimshaw, consultant to the Kerner Commission, "an unpopularity in-

Angry students constructed a barricade in Chicago's Grant Park against police and National Guardsmen who tried to prevent their demonstrations while the Democratic National Convention was in session. (*Wide World Photos*)

extricably tied up with their status as perceived economic and political threats to the 'older' immigrant groups."

When minority groups become strong and united enough, they may lash back at oppressors with riots of their own. Participation in such mobs is a means of expressing hostility, rebellion, and revenge, and of establishing pride of identity in a race, religion, or cult. Rioting gives traditional underdogs a new sense of power, an awareness that they can strike fear into the hearts of their dreaded enemies.

Most people who participate in mob violence belong to an "in-between" class—in between the privileged group above that oppresses them and an emerging group below that threatens them. Not daring to challenge the ruling class, they take out their frustrations, anxieties, and failures on the scapegoat class below.

Thus when Protestant workers in the cities were exploited by nineteenth-century industrialists, they rioted against newly arrived Catholics whom they saw as threatening their jobs. Similarly, when New York's Irish Catholics were exploited by a Protestant aristocracy, they vented their wrath in the Draft Riots of 1863 on black workers being brought in as strikebreakers to replace them.

In bad times, particularly, the in-between classes displace their anger at unemployment and other hardships on persons who are unable to strike back. "During periods of depression the number of lynchings is high," observed psychologists Carl I. Hovland and Robert R. Sears in a 1940 study. "During prosperity the number of lynchings declines."

In addition to hard times, any period of stress, strain, and upheaval is likely to produce riots, especially during wartime when large numbers of workers move from one part of the country to another for defense jobs, upsetting local balances of ethnic or racial groups. Minority groups may become victims of mob action, but may also riot themselves if the gap widens between what they expect and what they get.

Special circumstances influence whether a crowd turns into a rioting mob. The Kerner Report notes that most urban riots have begun between 7:00 P.M. and 12:30 A.M. on hot summer weekend nights, when the largest number of pedestrians are in the streets of the ghettos. In only a few cases has mass violence begun or continued in the daytime.

There must be a large enough crowd, as a rule, so that anonymity is reasonably assured. A Stanford University study indicates that people are twice as likely to resort to aggressive behavior when they are part of a mob. In a special study by social psychologists John Darley and Bibb Latané, it was found that in most street crises each bystander looks to others for silent guidance before acting.

"One person's violent reaction at the scene of a crime," they note, "may spread, through 'contagion,' to other members of the group." A few highly emotional people, shouting out bitter group grievances, can whip a crowd into a frenzy.

Whether a crowd turns into a mob often depends upon the handling of the situation by law enforcement agencies. When control measures are out of proportion to the disturbance, they can inflame counterviolence, as when demonstrators are beaten or shot instead of being arrested nonviolently. Matters are also worsened when the laws being enforced are considered unjust, or are enforced only against minority members.

Law enforcement agents may also be responsible for riots when they practice *under*control, making no effort to stop one group from violently attacking another, or doing so only after deliberate delay. Unwarranted delay in restoring order can magnify a street brawl into a full-scale riot.

The media bear a special responsibility in shaping both mob attitudes and actions. By reporting on minorities in an unfavorable way, the press, radio, and TV may reinforce prejudice and act as a goad to mob violence. Media coverage of a riot may also be inflammatory, spreading rumors or overplaying events for the sake of sensational news stories.

Matters are not helped, moreover, when TV viewers witness burning supermarkets, bricks shattering plate glass windows, streets turning into blazing battlegrounds. The public reacts with horror and demands stricter "law and order" measures. That in turn leads to overrepression, violations of civil liberties, and the outbreak of even greater rioting by oppressed minorities made desperate by persecution.

The riot in Watts was the first in which rioters were able to watch their own actions on TV. Continuous radio and TV coverage also gave them reports of police movements, so that they were better able to judge when and where it was safe to attack and loot stores.

The problem is a thorny one because while news reports may inadvertently worsen riots, the media still have a responsibility to keep the public honestly and fully informed. The line between good reportage and news coverage that inflames riots is one that cannot easily be drawn.

A brief word should be mentioned about mobs that are not hostile but too adoring—mobs of fans. They, too, can cause riots. When soul-singer James Brown gave a show in Los Angeles, his fans charged the stage. Police and firemen had to be called to break up a riot. In San Francisco Brown had to be locked in his dressing room to keep fans from mobbing him and tearing the clothes off his back for souvenirs.

In August 1926 one of the worst riots in the history of New York City erupted on Broadway when eighty thousand people, most of them women, fought each other and police to glimpse the silent movie star Rudolph Valentino as he lay in state in a Broadway funeral parlor. Hundreds were injured as mounted police, seeking to break up the riot, charged into the mob, and an emergency hospital had to be set up at the scene.

Such riots are worth studying along with more serious disturbances because they shed light on the role of mass hysteria in breakdowns of law and order.

In analyses of violent outbreaks, the role of rabblerousers and riot leaders is often overestimated, but there is no doubt that they do play a significant part. Sometimes they are highly placed politicians who seek to advance their own careers and ambitions with demagogic speeches intended to incite mob hostility toward minority groups. This tinder awaits only a spark for mass passions to burst into flame.

Similarly, street leaders can play on the grievances of a crowd and stir it into an ugly mood. Many urban riots were blamed on such spellbinding black leaders as Stokely Carmichael, Rap Brown, and Bobby Seale. Early in 1968 angry southern senators pushed an antiriot act through Congress to prevent them from crossing state lines to agitate.

A founder of Students for a Democratic Society (SDS) decried as simplistic this concept of the cause of urban uprisings. "Riots are much more than antisocial behavior," he pointed out. "Riots must be viewed both as a new stage in the development of Negro protest against racism, and as a logical outgrowth of the failure of the whole society to support racial equality. A riot represents people making history."

Riots may force Americans to face the injustices of their society. Labor riots in the early part of the twentieth century led eventually to the passage of the Wagner Act, labor's Magna Carta that compelled industrialists to bargain with labor unions. In this sense a series of riots may become the precursor of a new social movement for change.

New York Times correspondent Herbert L. Matthews noted that his paper had run an editorial called "The Failure of Violence" when the turbulent school year of 1968–1969 had ended. "It was not a convincing argument," he pointed out. "The upheaval at Columbia University, however ugly, had not failed. Important reforms followed, which would not otherwise have been made, or at least made in a foreseeable future."

Some authorities believe that no concessions should be made to mobs that riot, no matter how valid their grievances, because to legitimize or reward violence in this manner would undermine respect for law and order.

"I have always been taught," declared Supreme Court Justice Tom Clark, "that this nation was dedicated to freedom *under law,* not under mobs, whether they be integrationists or white secessionists. . . . For the Court to place its imprimatur upon [mobocracy] is a misfortune that those who love the law will always regret."

His son Ramsey Clark, the former attorney general, saw the problem in a different light. "From one side of America's house," he said, "we hear the demand for order: There must be order! It is the voice of those who resist change. From the other side of our house comes the plea for justice: Give us justice! This is the voice of those who seek change. But the long history of mankind says you will have neither order nor justice unless you have both."

President Johnson wrote of the year 1968, "Perhaps the most disturbing thing about the April riots was the fact that so many of us almost instinctively expected them to happen as soon as the news of Dr. King's death was made known. Were we becoming conditioned to violence? That prospect disturbed me far more than the initial shock of Watts or Detroit."

Is mob violence part of the American tradition?

"We must realize that violence has not been the action only of the roughnecks and racists among us," observes Prof. Richard M. Brown, College of William and Mary historian, "but has been the tactic of the most upright and respected of our people. . . . We have resorted so often to violence that we have long since become a 'trigger-happy' people."

Psychologist Sheldon G. Levy studied political violence over the last century and a half for the Kerner Commission. The record, he found, was "one of violence throughout American history. . . . [R]acial violence has been consistently high for the 150-year period. . . . The problem of violence in America is not new. By its very persistence it is a more serious problem for our society than it would be were it new, for its roots run very deep."

The Kerner Report pointed out, "One beneficent side effect of our current turmoil may be to force a harder and more candid look at our past."

When we do, notes Ramsey Clark, we will find that "few decades in our history are unscarred by riots."

3

Colonial Riots

A MOB OF four hundred Virginia backwoods tobacco growers rushed into Jamestown behind young Nathaniel Bacon. The frontiersmen were furious at Gov. William Berkeley for his pro-Indian policies, his failure to preserve law and order on the frontier, and his support of a tobacco monopoly. The year: 1676.

Surrounding the assembly then meeting in the state house, rioters flourished muskets at every window. The indignant governor went into the street and ripped open his tunic.

"Here!" he cried. "Shoot me! Before God—*shoot!*"

"No, it may please Your Honor," Bacon replied, "we will not hurt a hair of your head, nor of any other man's. We are come for a commission to save our lives from the Indians."

Taking over the assembly, he harangued it on the need for protection on the frontier. But the outraged assemblymen refused to authorize him to lead his own vigilante mob against the Indians. The rioters replied by putting the whole town to the torch, burning it to the ground.

When royal forces eventually recaptured Jamestown, the governor seized and hanged twenty-three of the mob under a decree of martial law. He was recalled to London by King Charles II, who observed wryly, "The old fool has hanged more people in that naked country than I did here for the murder of my father."

Bacon's rebellion propelled some changes. To calm down the frontiersmen, a subsequent Virginia assembly adopted many of the reform measures they demanded, and subsequent governors provided a readier ear to citizens' complaints.

Mobs often played an important role in civic elections. Colonial parties would use them to terrorize opponents away from the polls. One of the first election riots occurred in 1742 in the Pennsylvania colony, when Scotch-Irish frontiersmen who made up the Proprietary party sought to oust the Quakers for refusing to use force against Indians in the West.

They organized a mob of seventy sailors, arming them with clubs which they "flourished over their heads with loud huzzas, and in a furious and tumultuous manner approached the place of election." The polls were on a balcony of the courthouse, to which voters mounted from a street staircase.

Seizing and blocking the staircase, the mob clubbed and drove off all Quakers seeking to vote. But the ordinarily nonviolent Quakers quickly organized a huge mob of vigilantes who threw the sailors off the staircase and locked up fifty. The election then proceeded peacefully with a Quaker victory.

Hard-pressed farmers often felt compelled to form mobs to fight the edicts of courts controlled by wealthy landowners and merchants. In 1745 one mob of New Jersey tenant farmers crashed into the Newark jail that held Samuel Baldwin for refusing to pay rent to his landlord.

Like many tenant farmers, Baldwin insisted that he owned his land through purchase from its original owners, the Indians. The mob fought a bloody skirmish with jailors and took Baldwin off with it.

Three mob ringleaders were arrested for "high treason." When the sheriff of Essex and his deputies sought to bring one to court for trial, the mob attacked and drove them off, rescuing the prisoner. The rioters then marched on the jail to demand the release of the other two. Militiamen barred their way with raised firelocks, loaded and cocked, as a justice read out King George's proclamation against riots.

Crying defiance, the mob charged with swinging clubs through flying lead. Men on both sides were wounded. Sweeping aside the soldiers, the farmers surged into the prison and felled the sheriff, who tried to hold them off with a sword. The prison door was broken open with an ax and the prisoners were carried off by the jubilant mob.

Its success inspired a whole decade of tenant riots against eviction and imprisonment, finally compelling royal governors to stop acting as agents for the landlords.

One of the most persistent complaints of Americans against His Majesty's navy was the seizure and impressment of seamen by "press gangs" in the ports. In 1747, after a fresh batch had been shanghaied in Boston, an angry mob raged through the streets wielding clubs and cutlasses. Three naval officers who crossed its path were seized, roped, and held as hostages to exchange for the impressed seamen.

By a ruse Gov. William Shirley managed to free the British officers, whereupon the mob attacked the General Court with stones and bricks. After breaking in, rioters warned frightened council members that unless Como. Charles Knowles released the impressed seamen, blood would flow. Capturing a royal barge, the mob bore it to the commons and burned it.

The outraged commodore threatened to bring his whole squadron into port next morning and turn his guns on the defiant Bostonians, but Governor Shirley dissuaded him. Next day the mob smashed into private homes to capture five petty officers as new hostages. When Shirley ordered out the militia to suppress the riot, the militiamen refused and many joined the mob as it marched upon Shirley's house.

The governor fled to Castle William. The uproar refused to die down until the crown won the release of the captured officers by conceding that there would be no further impressment of seamen in Boston Harbor. Press gangs continued to function in other ports, however, provoking other anitnavy explosions like the Knowles Riot of 1747.

Colonial mobs of vigilantes frequently vented their fury on Indians, attacking peaceful as well as warlike tribes on the theory that "an Indian is an Indian."

The Conestogas of Pennsylvania were a Christianized tribe who sold brooms and baskets to the Quakers and who had welcomed William Penn with a treaty of friendship for "as long as the sun should shine, or the waters run in the rivers."

Just before a frosty dawn in the winter of 1763, six Conestogas—three men, two women, a young boy—lay asleep in their village near Lancaster on the frontier, when they were awakened by bloodcurdling yells. A mob of frontiersmen from the small town of Paxton fell upon them with firelocks, cutlasses, and hatchets. The "Paxton boys" then scalped their victims, mangled their bodies, and set fire to all the huts in the village.

The fourteen villagers who had been away during the massacre appealed in terror to Gov. John Penn for protection, and were sheltered in Lancaster's sturdily built jail. Hearing of this, the Paxton mob galloped to Lancaster and smashed into the jail. The Indians fell to their knees begging for mercy, but all were slaughtered.

An outraged Benjamin Franklin wrote a tract to arouse fellow Pennsylvanians against such lawless mobs: "The barbarous men who committed the atrocious act, in defiance of government, of all laws human and divine, and to the eternal disgrace of their country and colour, then mounted their horses, huzza'd in triumph, as if they had gained a victory, and rode off—*unmolested*! . . . THE BLOOD OF THE INNOCENT WILL CRY TO HEAVEN FOR VENGEANCE." At the head of a militia, he prevented the Paxton mob from massacring more Christianized Indians, the Moravians, who were being sheltered in Philadelphia.

But as the frontier moved steadily west, the fanatical hatred that the Paxton mob had vented on the Conestogas in 1763 was a grim omen for all native Americans.

The early resistance to British tyranny that led to the American Revolution was largely the work of mobs organized by the anti-British Sons of Liberty. When the first stamps for use in the new stamp tax on all legal papers, bills, and newspapers arrived in New York, thousands of New Yorkers turned out on November 1, 1765, for a protest demonstration.

Frightened by the roaring crowds in the streets, Acting Governor Cadwallader Colden took refuge with the stamps in Fort George. As the demonstrators swarmed around the fort, Colden ordered Gen. Thomas Gage to lower the black muzzles of the fort's cannon. The Sons of Liberty sent him a warning that if the guns were fired on citizens, he and Gage would be lynched. Colden refused their demand for the stamps.

The crowd erected a gibbet and hanged him in effigy. Not yet a mob, the demonstrators were in a carnival mood.

Forming a torchlight procession, they carried scaffold and effigy down Broadway, shouting for all New Yorkers to join them.

Barrels of rum soon turned the celebrants into a wild mob. Assaulting the governor's carriage-house, they dragged out his elegant coach and sleigh. These were thrown on a huge bonfire built of fence palings. The mob next broke into the beautiful home of a Royal Artillery major, smashed the elegant furniture, demolished a priceless library and works of art, and ruined his gardens.

When the new governor arrived to replace Colden, he discreetly gave up any intention of enforcing the stamp act. He also appeased New Yorkers by dismantling Fort George's guns.

In 1765 New Yorkers protested a new stamp tax by forming a torchlight procession that turned into a destructive mob before the demonstrations subsided. (*Culver Pictures*)

The New York antistamp riot, and those organized by the Sons of Liberty in other cities, convinced Parliament that the obnoxious tax had to be repealed. Overjoyed Americans celebrated with victory bonfires. Rioters were held in new respect as bold patriots who could force the arrogant British empire to back down in its mistreatment of the colonies.

Race riots, which have characterized much of the mob violence that studs American history, also had their origins in the period before the Revolution. One of the earliest took place in 1712 in a New York City that was then largely farmland with only a half dozen paved streets and no sidewalks. Of the ten thousand population, 20 percent consisted of black slaves, most of whom were cruelly treated by their masters.

On April 6 twenty-three slaves gathered secretly after midnight outside the house of Peter Van Tilburgh, whose house was to be set ablaze to signal to the two thousand blacks of the city that an uprising against white New Yorkers had begun. The plan whispered around called for all slaves to join the arsonists quickly, lie in ambush around the house, and slay all the whites who came running to put the fire out.

A torch was flung. As the house went up in flames, an alarm roused white New Yorkers who tumbled out of bed and raced through the muddy streets. The first to reach the fire stared in amazement at the blacks silhouetted against the flames. The slaves were armed with guns, long knives, and hatchets they had secured from drunken crews off the vessels in port.

Opening fire, they rushed upon the whites with uplifted blades, killing several. Other whites fled to the Battery fort and roused the governor, who ordered the cannon to be fired. The crash of the shot shook every New Yorker awake. Seeing the flames, many rushed to join the firefighters.

The slaves were now a large mob. Nine whites had been killed, and many wounded lay groaning on the earth, by the time the governor's soldiers arrived with bayonets drawn. The rioters fired a final volley, then fled north into the darkness, making for the woods and swamps.

Pursued by soldiers and white civilians, some were caught and slain on the spot. Others, surrounded and cut off in thickets, were seized by dawn's light. Some trapped slaves turned their guns and knives on themselves in terror.

A swift trial sentenced twenty-one black prisoners to die. As a grim warning to other slaves, some were hanged, some tortured and broken on the wheel, some burned to death. One sadistic sentence called for the victim to be "burned with a slow fire that he may continue in torment for eight or ten hours and continue burning in the said fire until he be dead and consumed to ashes."

In 1741 rumors that another slave revolt would erupt on the thirtieth anniversary of the first uprising spread panic among New Yorkers. A series of fires that had broken out were attributed to vengeful blacks who had been captured with a Spanish crew and sold as slaves at auction.

A Mrs. Earle of Broadway reported to an alderman that when two Spanish blacks had passed her window, she had heard one laugh, "Fire! Fire! Scorch! Scorch!" Rumors flashed around the city that the slaves were planning to burn down the city and poison the water supply. Thousands of frightened New Yorkers began fleeing north to the country in hired carts and vehicles. In a desperate effort to net plotters, slaves of all ages and sexes were arrested.

The witch-hunt went on for three months, with at least one new victim condemned every day. Eighteen were hanged, including a Catholic priest charged with complicity; thirteen were burned alive at the stake; and over seventy were transported to other countries.

When the panic finally subsided, a nervous New York assembly imposed a high tax on the importation of any more slaves. New Yorkers breathed a sigh of relief that they no longer had to fear for their lives at the hands of a "slave mob." The slaves of New York wondered when they would next have to fear for their own lives at the hands of a white mob.

There were other slave riots, real or imaginary, that were put down bloodily. Leaders, real or suspected, were punished with a savagery that made white claims to be "the civilized race" an ironic joke among slaves. And in each case mobs of white citizens cheered the executions, never doubting that justice was being done, seldom questioning injustices that provoked slaves to fight and die for freedom.

4

Mobs of the American Revolution

"THERE'S TWO OF the lobster scoundrels! Get them!"

An angry mob of Boston workers pounced on two British redcoats encountered in the streets after dark on March 5, 1770, beating them savagely. That would teach them to take after-hour jobs away from American workers who needed them!

The commotion brought forty redcoats to the aid of their assaulted comrades. Driving off the workers, the soldiers swarmed through the streets insulting, abusing, and shoving all Bostonians in their path. Someone rang fire bells in two meeting-houses, bringing an outpouring of citizens.

"I saw the people in great commotion," later testified the commander of the guard, a captain named Preston, "and heard them use the most cruel and horrid threats against the troops. . . . They immediately surrounded the sentinel posted (at the custom-house), and with clubs and other weapons threatened to execute their vengeance on him."

Preston posted eight redcoats in a semicircle around the custom-house armed with loaded firelocks and fixed bayonets to hold off the mob. Rioters taunted the soldiers. One jeered, "Come on, you rascals, you bloody backs, you lobster scoundrels—fire if you dare!" The soldiers drove them back with bayonet thrusts. Henry Knox, later Washington's secretary of war, approached Preston to protest.

The mob began hurling snowballs and pieces of ice. Preston, who later claimed that he and a soldier had been hit by clubs, gave the order to fire. Up to a dozen shots rang out, killing five colonists and wounding six. The rioters fled.

An infuriated mob of five thousand bore down on the redcoats' barracks, but was forced to halt in the face of the leveled guns of a whole regiment in King Street. The mob dispersed only upon the lieutenant governor's promise that those responsible for the shootings would be brought to trial.

When Captain Preston and his eight guards were tried before a Boston jury, they were defended by a future president, John Adams. The jury exonerated all but two soldiers, who were found guilty of manslaughter and were punished by branding on the hand.

A riot that had begun as a street brawl was skillfully magnified by Sam Adams and his Sons of Liberty into the inflammatory designation of "the Boston Massacre," to agitate Americans toward full-scale revolution against the British.

Mobs rioted against the British with increasing frequency in the six years before the Revolution.

One of the most celebrated mobs in American history ran riot at the end of 1773 when the tea ships arrived in Boston Harbor from England. The riot was secretly planned by rabblerouser Sam Adams, who enlisted the aid of Ebenezer MacKintosh, leader of the South End Mob, waterfront thugs whom the Sons of Liberty often used to create anti-British commotions.

At a town meeting in the Old South Church on the night of December 16, Adams and John Hancock demanded that Gov. Thomas Hutchinson order the ships to take the tea back to England and insist the Parliament rescind its tea tax. Upon Hutchinson's refusal, Adams told the jammed hall, "This meeting can do nothing further to save the country." Hancock shouted, "Let every man do what is right in his own eyes!"

On signal the South End Mob, disguised as Mohawk Indians and blacks, stormed past the building toward the wharf. Crowds from the hall raced after them to the port, where all swarmed over one of the tea ships. Breaking open 342 big chests of tea, the rioters dumped them into the harbor, crying jubilantly, "Boston Harbor a teapot tonight!"

The Boston Tea Party provoked the overreaction that crafty Sam Adams had counted upon—Parliament's passage of the Boston Port Act, which shut down the harbor until Bostonians agreed to pay for the dumped tea, and the Quartering Act, which allowed the royal governor to take over private houses for quartering soldiers. So the mob action of "patriots" helped make conciliation between crown and colonies impossible.

Once the Revolution broke out, Tories or Loyalists—who only a day earlier had enjoyed the status of respectable, law-abiding citizens—found themselves the targets of violent Whig patriot mobs as "traitors."

In a letter to England, Ann Hulton, a Boston official's wife, described one mob's lynching of an aged Tory named Malcolm: "He was stript stark naked, one of the severest cold nights this winter, his body coverd all over with tar, then with feathers, his arm dislocated in tearing off his cloaths, he dragged in a cart with thousands attending, some beating him with clubs & knocking him out of the cart, then in again. They gave him several severe whippings, at different parts of the town. This spectacle of horror & sportive cruelty was exhibited for about five hours. . . . When under torture they demanded of him to curse his masters the K: Gov &c which they could not make him do, but he still cried, 'Curse all traitors.' They brought him to the gallows & put a rope about his neck saying they would hang him. . . . The doctors say that it is impossible this poor creature can live."

Wealthy conservatives often suffered mobbing as suspected Tory sympathizers. After the British had been forced to evacuate Philadelphia in 1779, a vengeful mob bearing torches set upon the house of James Wilson, a signer of the Declaration who had acted as a lawyer for the Tories.

Wilson barricaded himself in the house with armed friends, one of whom opened a window and waved a pistol at the gathered mob. Shots were exchanged and he was killed. A full-scale battle erupted with casualties on both sides. Philadelphia's chief executive, Gen. Joseph Reed, galloped to the scene at the head of the city's light-horse cavalry.

Charging horses scattered the mob, and twenty-seven rioters were arrested. But when another mob threatened to storm the jail, they were set free on bail. The assembly, holding the riot to be a product of the passions of war, decided to issue an act of amnesty to all involved.

In the woods of New Jersey, mobs of Whigs and Tories raided each other, while in North Carolina and Georgia mobs on both sides took, tortured, and hanged prisoners.

The end of the war saw the formation of mobs of veterans angered by returning home to unplowed land and mounting debts, their pockets stuffed with worthless paper money. They pleaded in vain with the courts to suspend judgments that were forfeiting their farms, sending some to prison for debt, and even selling others into servitude to pay off creditors.

In Massachusetts one bankrupt veteran, Capt. Daniel Shays, led a mob of bitter farmers into Northampton in 1786 to shut down the courthouse by force. Following their success, they were eagerly joined by a thousand more in seizing and burning other courthouses and beating up government officials.

"For God's sake, tell me, what is the cause of these commotions," demanded a baffled George Washington at Mount Vernon. "If they have *real* grievances, redress them if possible. If they have not, employ the force of government against them at once."

In December 1787 Shays's mob shut down the Springfield courts, then headed for the city arsenal defended by Maj. Gen. William Shepherd. Warning the rioters to disperse, Shepherd commanded his artillery to fire warning shots over their heads. Roaring with anger, the mob charged. The soldiers lowered their sights and killed four men.

"Murder! Murder!" screamed the rioters. Fleeing to the countryside, they were pursued by troops, who captured 150. Several were threatened with hanging, but all were eventually released. Shays escaped to Vermont and was granted a pardon in the general amnesty passed in 1788.

Widespread sympathy for Shays's Rebellion swept Gov. James Bowdoin out of office for having called out state troops against the rioters. In the landslide that made John Hancock governor, some members of Shay's mob were elected legislators.

Bowdoin had appealed to Congress for help against the rioters, but Congress had been unable to respond because it lacked power under the Articles of Confederation. This was a factor in calling a constitutional convention in Philadelphia over bitter opposition by many Americans who feared the growth of a centralized tyranny.

"Mob violence threatened the Constitutional Convention in Philadelphia in 1787," noted Ramsey Clark, "causing that convention to provide in the Constitution itself for a federal place of government . . . to safely conduct the activities of the new republic."

Thousands of burials of fallen veterans of the Revolution had made the nation freshly conscious of the solemnity of death and the sacredness of cemeteries. When New Yorkers discovered in 1788 that medical students were robbing graves—"body-snatching"—for the purpose of dissection to learn anatomy, they rioted in outrage.

The spark was a gruesome practical joke played by an insensitive young surgeon of Columbia Hospital. Displaying a human arm to some children playing outside, he told one boy it was his mother's. The shocked boy, whose mother had recently died, rushed home in tears to his father, a mason. The mason had his wife's grave opened and found the body gone.

When his fellow workers heard about it, they seized their tools and marched furiously on the city hospital. The news spread swiftly, and they were joined by dozens, then hundreds, then over a thousand incensed New Yorkers. Bursting into the hospital, they smashed equipment and attacked medical students.

The mayor rushed to the hospital with the sheriff, who appeased the mob by taking students and doctors off to jail. But by evening the city was in an uproar. A huge new mob descended on the hospital to lynch any doctors and medical students it could lay hands upon. Finding none, it broke into Columbia College and doctors' houses searching for victims.

Learning that all medical personnel had been whisked to prison to protect them, the frustrated hordes rushed to the jail shrieking, "Bring out your doctors!" Alarmed city authorities called out the militia, but they were driven off with a hail of paving-stones, their guns seized and smashed.

Rioters flung themselves at the jail doors to batter them down. Failing, they smashed windows and sought to scramble in. Doctors, medical students, and guards clubbed them back. New York's governor, mayor, and several important civic leaders rushed to the jail to plead for calm, accompanied by a new and larger force of militia.

Advancing on the mob with drawn bayonets, the soldiers were met with a volley of stones and brickbats. John Jay, secretary for foreign affairs, was hit on the head and seriously hurt. When the governor decided to order the troops to open fire, he was entreated not to by revolutionary hero Baron Friedrich von Steuben. A hurled stone knocked Steuben down. From the ground, his temperance evaporated, Steuben cried out wrathfully, "Fire, Governor, fire!" The order was given.

A white flash lit up the dark street. The stunned mob, not believing it would actually be fired upon, froze in a statuelike tableau. The militia fired again. New Yorkers fell, groaning in anguish. Panic swept the mob, which now turned and fled into the night in every direction.

Public indignation ran so high that for a while the authorities feared a general revolt. Threats against physicians and medical students frightened many out of the city. Mob passions were impervious to medical pleading that dissection was vital to the training of the doctors New Yorkers depended upon to rescue themselves and their families from pain and disease.

Poor farmers who had dropped their pitchforks for guns to fight against King George's unfair taxes were incensed when Treasury Secretary Alexander Hamilton imposed a 25 percent excise tax on whiskey. Many small farmers in remote areas could not get their grain to market except by distilling it in the form of rye whiskey.

Hamilton's tax had three purposes: to raise money to pay off the federal government's creditors; to assert the power of the central government over states and regions; and to discourage excessive drinking.

When tax collectors and process servers invaded the rural

regions of Pennsylvania, New York, North Carolina, Virginia, and the Ohio valley, they were driven out by mobs of infuriated farmers. Government officials' homes were broken into, looted, and burned. Farmers who submitted to paying the whiskey tax were mobbed and tarred and feathered.

A Philadelphia court gave tax inspector John Neville subpoenas to serve against thirty-seven balky farmers in western Pennsylvania. He was driven off on July 17, 1794, by an enraged mob of five hundred farmers led by James McFarlane. The mob then surged to his house, but found that he had fled.

The occupants of the house, Neville's relatives and eleven federal soldiers, were given an ultimatum by McFarlane: "Surrender the house, or surrender the subpoenas—one or the other must be burned!" Rebuffed, the mob opened fire, which was returned. McFarlane was killed; three soldiers and some rioters were wounded. The mob forced those in the house to surrender, then put it to the torch.

Three weeks later a mob of ten thousand agitated farmers threatened to attack the courts in Pittsburgh. That city's officials hastily promised that the whiskey tax would not be enforced. Federal authorities grew alarmed that the Whisky Rebellion might spread into a united uprising.

"Shall the majority govern or be governed?" demanded Hamilton indignantly. Washington branded the attack on Neville's house an act of treason and ordered all rioters to disband. "The very existence of government and the fundamental principles of social order are materially involved," he warned.

When the rebel farmers persisted in their defiance, Hamilton urged Washington to act quickly to demonstrate federal authority over the states. At the advance of an army of thirteen thousand men, the mobs quickly melted away and the revolt collapsed. Twenty prisoners were taken and marched to trial, but only two were found guilty of high treason. Washington pardoned both, one as a "simpleton," and the other as "insane."

Bitterly criticized for an excessive show of force, Hamilton insisted that a lesser force would have permitted a riot to become an insurrection. " 'Tis better far to err on the other side," he maintained. "When the government appears in arms, it ought to apear like a Hercules, and inspire respect by the display of strength."

That same year when he attempted to make a political speech from a balcony in Wall Street, he was roared down by an angry crowd and hit by flying stones. Blood streaming from his face, Hamilton told his opponents bitterly, "If you use such knockdown arguments, I must retire."

The rioting mobs of Shays's Rebellion and the Whisky Rebellion had mirrored the dissatisfaction of the broad masses of Americans with an elitist Federalist rule. Failing to heed the warning, the Federalists were swept out of power in 1800 by Jefferson's Republicans.

5

Rise of the Vigilantes

FEDERALISTS AGAIN FOUND themselves the target of Jeffersonian mobs in 1812, when they protested President James Madison's declaration of war on the British. Ultrapatriotic rioters burst into the homes of Federalist editors, destroyed their presses, and drove them out of town.

In Baltimore when a mob brought up a cannon in front of one editor's house, Federalist defenders within opened fire, killing and wounding some attackers. The Federalists were temporarily saved from the wrath of the mob by cavalry, which swept them off to jail. But the mob thundered after them, smashing into the jail.

When Gen. Henry Lee, father of Robert E. Lee, tried to stop the mob he was battered so savagely that he could neither talk nor eat solid food for two months. The mob then seized and tortured the prisoners, afterward beating them insensible.

Federalist fears that unrestrained democracy would lead to "mobocracy" seemed to have come true on the occasion of Andrew Jackson's inauguration as president. On March 4, 1829, over twenty thousand Americans swarmed into Washington to celebrate with the "People's President." Daniel Webster described them as "a monstrous crowd."

To demonstrate that his administration would represent the common man, not the vested interests, Jackson invited the crowds to have refreshments on the lawn of the White House.

"What a scene did we witness!" reported Mrs. Margaret Bayard Smith, a Washington matron. ". . . Cut glass and china to the amount of several thousand dollars had been broken in the struggle to get the refreshments. . . . Ladies fainted, men were seen with bloody noses and such a scene of confusion took place as is impossible to describe,—those who got in could not get out by the door again, but had to scramble out of windows."

The president had been "nearly pressed to death and almost suffocated and torn to pieces by the people," and had fled out a back way. "It was the People's day. . . . Of all tyrants, they are the most ferocious, cruel and despotic."

The rapid growth of industry between 1830 and 1860 filled the cities of the Northeast with masses of Irish immigrant workers. In the four cities of Baltimore, Philadelphia, New York, and Boston alone, some thirty-five major anti-Catholic riots took place during this era. Mobs of Protestant workers, who felt threatened by the willingness of the Irish to work long hours for low wages, wrecked the immigrants' homes and neighborhoods.

Mob passions were inflamed by an ignorant bigotry that branded Catholicism "un-American," charging that it was just a smoke screen for a Vatican plot to take over the United States. Widely circulated books spread gruesome tales about "works of the devil" that went on in convents.

William L. Stone, respected publisher of the New York *Commercial Advertiser*, led an investigation of charges made in one lurid best seller, *Six Months In a Convent: Awful Disclosures of Maria Monk*. "What nonsense," he reported, "and how great the popular credulity to swallow it!" But it inflamed mobs into burning convent buildings, stoning Catholic homes, and attacking Irish workers in street brawls.

One of the worst such riots occurred in 1834 in the Charlestown area of Boston. It was sparked by a spiteful scullery maid in the kitchen of the Ursuline convent who sought revenge when her bid to become a nun was turned down. Posing as an "escaped nun," she told a sensational story of being forced to take orders against her will, and of other captive nuns and insubordinate pupils being held and abused in dark "vaults" under the convent boarding school.

Posters sprang up around Boston and Charlestown: "To Arms!! To Arms!! Ye brave and free, the avenging sword unshield!! Leave not one stone upon another of that curst Nunnery!!"

By an unfortunate coincidence, a nun known as Sister Joan had suffered a breakdown from overwork, left the Ursuline convent briefly to board with family friends, then recovered and returned. Rumors spread that she had been imprisoned in the convent crypt, had escaped, then had been recaptured.

The Charlestown selectmen bowed to popular pressure and sent a committee of five to the convent to investigate. They were presented to Sister Joan, who explained the truth and also showed them through the institution's cellars. But before they could publish their findings, violence erupted.

On the night of August 11, a mob of workingmen swarmed to the convent howling, "Free the prisoners!"

"I heard—what shall I call it?—a shout, a cry, a howl, a yell," recollected Louisa Goddard, one of the schoolgirls asleep in the convent school dormitory. "It was the sound of a mob, a voice of the night, indeed, that made it hideous. . . . The mob gave one roar as it crossed Charlestown Bridge and then observed profound silence till it reached the convent grounds. My heart beat thick and fast. . . .

"A horrible yell suddently rent the air within a few yards of the windows at which I was standing, and a host of dark figures rushed into view. I flew across the room to Elizabeth Williams's bed, shaking her and crying out, 'Wake up, wake up, the mob has really come!' She started up screaming. All the girls in the dormitory suddenly wakened, screaming in concert, 'O, the mob, the mob,—we shall all be killed!' "

The mob leaders pounded on the door. "Produce the miserable victims you're holding prisoner in the dungeons!"

Confronting them, Mother St. George, the mother superior, said icily that the selectmen had already investigated the rumors and declared them false. Mob leaders demanded that she step aside and let the mob search for itself.

"Disperse immediately!" she cried angrily. "For if you don't the bishop has twenty thousand Irishmen at his command in Boston, and they will whip you all into the sea!"

At this the mob exploded wrathfully and began hurling stones. Two shots were fired. Mother St. George slammed the doors shut and bolted them. The rioters withdrew briefly to build a bonfire of tar barrels—the signal to summon supporters from all over Charlestown. The mob quickly swelled to four thousand. Ringleaders broached a hogshead of rum; drunken war cries soon rent the night. Seizing torches at midnight, mob leaders led a howling horde in storming the convent.

Mother St. George hurried to the dormitory, gathered the children and nuns, and led them quickly out of the building through a back entrance to a sheltered garden.

Smashing windows, men climbed inside and overran the convent from garret to cellar. They vandalized furniture, books, and religious objects, and made bonfires of them in several rooms. Musical instruments were hurled out the

51

windows. Some of the mob looted silverware. Others dashed from room to room setting fire to drapes.

"Get the mother superior! Burn the old witch!"

Mother St. George, the nuns, and children in the garden huddled together in terrified silence as rioters ran about searching for them. Under cover of darkness, a rescuer tore palings off the fence enclosure and helped them escape. Three children later died from the effects of exposure and shock.

Fire bells clanged all over Charlestown, Boston, and Cambridge. Eleven companies answered the alarms, but the mob cut their hoses, threatening to assault any firemen who attempted to save the convent.

Boston Mayor Theodore Lyman, Jr., called a town meeting in Faneuil Hall to denounce the riot as a "base and cowardly act." An investigation led to the arrest of thirteen rioters on charges of arson, a crime punishable by death. But when the defendants were tried in Concord, mobs surged on the court threatening witnesses, judge, and jury if a verdict of guilty was found. Court officers were hanged in effigy.

All defendants but one teen-ager were freed, cheered as heroes as they left court, and honored with fifty-gun salutes. The teen-ager was soon pardoned by the governor. The Massachusetts legislature refused to indemnify the Ursuline convent. Mob spirit had triumphed over religious liberty in Boston. As a silent reproach, the Catholic community let the ruins of the convent stand for fifty years.

A different kind of mob sprang up in the 1830s in the lower southern states, particularly along the Mississippi, where riverboats deposited gamblers, robbers, horse thieves, counterfeiters, and desperadoes. Many unsavory characters menaced the peace of towns they settled in, but were often too shrewd to fall afoul of the law. In despair local citizens organized vigilante committees to take the law into their own hands, hoping to frighten undesirables out of the community.

Typical was the vigilante mob that sought to drive gambling houses and gamblers from Vicksburg, Mississippi, in 1835. Seizing one gambler, the vigilantes whipped him, covered him with tar and feathers, and gave him forty-eight hours to get out of town. A posted notice warned other gamblers of similar treatment if they remained in Vicksburg.

Two days later a mob of several hundred vigilantes broke into all the gambling houses of the city, confiscating faro tables and other equipment. In one house shots rang out from the darkened interior, killing a vigilante. The mob returned the fire, then burst in and overpowered five gamblers with guns. All were immediately "executed"—the vigilante euphemism for murder. Then all the confiscated equipment was thrown on a victory bonfire to celebrate the "clean-up."

The vigilante movement moved west with the frontier, which attracted the lawless along with the pioneer. Vigilante mobs were usually led by the "better" elements of a community who, in the absence of dependable law and order forces, felt justified in organizing mob action against "bad men."

The leaders were often men ambitious to establish their positions as community pillars, for business or political advantage. Most mob members were men of property anxious to protect it against outlaws or horse and cattle thieves by making theft a hanging offense. The mobs sometimes gave a patina of legality to their lynching bees by holding informal "trials," at which a parody of justice was meted out to victims. Accusation was tantamount to conviction and execution.

In 1837 a future president warned against the vigilante

spirit. Young Abe Lincoln castigated "the increasing disregard for law which pervades the country—the growing disposition to substitute the wild and furious passions in lieu of the sober judgments of courts, and the worse than savage mobs for the executive ministers of justice."

Because of the dangers, terrors, and excesses of the frontier, almost everyone carried guns, so that vigilantes were always armed mobs. Critics of today's high level of armed violence in the United States attribute it largely to the tradition of the "gun culture" that developed in the West and was made respectable by the vigilantes.

In 1837 the New York *Commercial Register* grimly reminded its affluent readers that the French Revolution had begun with "mobs clamoring for bread, marching in procession, and committing outrages against the bakers." The occasion of this reminder was the startling Flour Riot, which broke out in the wake of a financial panic that made two hundred thousand New York workers jobless and sent food prices soaring.

Poor working-class families found themselves unable to afford even bread when the price of flour almost doubled to twelve dollars a barrel. Five thousand poorly clad New Yorkers braved the February cold to attend a protest meeting in front of City Hall. Angry speakers cried out against greedy businesses like Hart & Company, a large wholesaler rumored to be hoarding hugh stores of flour and wheat in its warehouse, for seeking to make big profits out of the suffering of the poor.

At the urging of one agitator, a thousand shouting men charged down Broadway to attack Hart's warehouse. Forcing their way in, they seized hundreds of barrels of flour and rolled them out into the street. Spilling from the smashed barrels, the flour turned rioters' clothes and faces a ghostly white. Thousands of bushels of wheat were also pitched to the pavement.

Police charged rioters through the ankle-deep flour, but were overwhelmed and their nightsticks captured. New York's mayor, arriving with the rest of the mob from the park, begged the rioters to go home. He was driven off with a hail of bricks and chunks of ice. Flour was now everywhere. Women scooped it up into boxes, baskets, and aprons, hurrying home with the white treasure to their families.

As night fell fresh detachments of police arrived, along with troops. Several rioters were arrested, but the mob pursued and attacked the police, freeing the prisoners. Other rioters attacked another major flour merchant's premises, spilling thirty barrels until he won immunity by pledging to give all his flour on hand to the poor.

The Flour Riot frightened wealthy Americans, who saw it as a possible forerunner of a new revolution that would pit the poor masses against the prosperous few. Worried socialites began organizing concerts and balls to raise funds among the affluent for relief of the poor, until hard times had run their course by 1843.

During the 1840s Protestant workingmen, resentful of Catholic progress in winning better jobs and political clout, organized the Native Americans. They acquired the derisive nickname of "Know-Nothings," after the reply they gave when questioned about their violent anti-Catholic activities.

In 1844 mobs of Know-Nothings fought bloody street battles with the Irish of Philadelphia, attacking and burning Catholic schools, churches, homes, and stores for almost a week. A cavalry charge finally routed them after two soldiers had been killed and twenty-six wounded, with a greater toll among the rioters. For weeks afterward troops had to be kept on guard at every Catholic church in Philadelphia.

The Mormons, founded by Joseph Smith in western New York, were also victimized by intolerant mobs. Fiercely resented for their practice of polygamy, they were also considered to be "in league with the Devil" because their hard-working communities always prospered. Driven out by mobs in New York, Ohio, and Missouri, they fled to Carthage, Illinois, where another mob killed Smith. When Mormon leadership passed to Brigham Young, he led his followers to Salt Lake City, Utah, where they finally found refuge from mob persecution.

As Democrats succeeded in organizing the immigrant vote in the big cities, the Native Americans intensified their efforts to keep foreign-born voters from the polls. The immigrants fought back. Killings on election day were commonplace during the 1840s and 1850s. The worst of election riots took place in St. Louis, Missouri, in August 1854.

Know-Nothings spread rumors that the Irish were stacking arms in St. Patrick's Church, and that an Irishman had stabbed a Native American in the back. Neither rumor was true, but a mob armed with axes attacked rows of Irish houses, demolishing sixty. A quickly formed Irish mob fought back.

"For forty-eight hours," reported a St. Louis newspaper, "the city has been the scene of one of the most appalling riots that has ever taken place in the country. Men have been butchered like cattle, property destroyed and anarchy reigns supreme. . . . The military and police have, thus far, been unable to check the onward march of lawlessness and crime. The scenes of last night were terrible, never, we hope, to be enacted again." Ten had been killed, thirty seriously wounded.

In Louisville, Kentucky, the following year, Know-Nothing mobs took control of the polls, beating, shooting, and stabbing Irish and German immigrants who sought to vote. When some Irish killed several rioters, enraged mobs invaded their neighborhoods, burned buildings, and shot down fleeing tenants.

Twenty people died. Know-Nothing candidates swept the elections, with almost no Irish or German votes recorded.

In 1856 the Native Americans elected governors in nine states and sent 112 members to Congress. Abe Lincoln wrote wryly from Springfield, "As a nation we began by declaring that 'all men are created equal.' We now practically read it, 'all men are created equal except Negroes.' When the Know-Nothings obtain control, it will read: 'All men are created equal except Negroes, foreigners, and Catholics.' "

During this era, in many parts of the South and West the law of the mob prevailed—lynch law, so-called because a Virginia Whig, Col. Charles Lynch, had led vigilantes in seizing and whipping Tories during the Revolution. By the middle of the nineteenth century, murder by hanging had replaced whipping as the punishment inflicted by lynch mobs.

Texas led all states in lynching, boasting of fifty-two different vigilante movements. "In this lawless region," one visitor to the Texas frontier observed, "men were seldom convicted of homicide, and never punished. . . . If you want distinction in this country, kill somebody."

Frontier regions could seldom afford adequate police, court, or prison systems. In many areas outlaws charged with crimes were able to ensure acquittal by bribes or threats. Frontiersmen generally supported vigilantes as providing a swift and sure, if crude, brand of justice.

In California the gold rush brought a large criminal element to the mining camps and boomtown San Francisco. Hoodlums robbed and killed at will. Fearing to be on San

Francisco's streets after dark, citizens barricaded their doors and windows when the sun went down. Over a thousand murders occurred between 1849 and 1856, with only one conviction.

Convictions were rare because witnesses were intimidated, and police, officials, and courts were corrupted by bribery and political influence. Control of the city was in the hands of an Irish Democratic machine that had a vested interest in crime and rackets. Rebellious public feeling was sparked by middle- and upper-class Protestants, many of them former Whigs and Know-Nothings from the Northeast.

On June 10, 1851, an ex-convict named Jenkins was caught red-handed making off with a merchant's safe. San Francisco merchants organized a committee of vigilance. Holding a kangaroo court, they sentenced Jenkins to hang and rang a fire bell to summon citizens at 2:00 A.M. and announce the news.

The crowd roared approval. Jenkins was then taken to a nearby adobe house. Fastening a rope around his neck, vigilante leader Sam Brannan threw the other end over a projecting wooden beam and shouted, "Every lover of liberty and good order lay hold of this rope!" The mob did.

Subsequently the vigilantes seized ninety-one other hoodlums; they hanged some and drove the others out of town. Impressed, other California cities emulated San Francisco's example and organized their own committees of vigilance.

At Downieville in July 1851 a drunken Californian named Joseph Cannon broke into the home of a Mexican woman known only as Juanita, who stabbed him in self-defense. Vigilantes seized her and held court in the town plaza. Finding her guilty of having murdered one of the town's "most popular citizens," the mob took her to a bridge where she was ordered to put a noose around her own neck, then hanged from a bridge beam.

Vigilante groups were usually organized by businessmen anxious to protect property while paying less taxes for the costs of imprisonment, court trials, and executions. In 1858 a mounted vigilante troop calling themselves "Regulators," who paraded under a banner reading "Regulators—no expense to the County," issued a justification of their lynch law in northern Indiana.

"The people of this country are the real sovereigns," they insisted, "and whenever the laws . . . are found inadequate to their protection, it is the right of the people to take the protection of their property into their own hands, and deal with these villains according to their just desserts."

On the gold fields of Montana, the law was Sheriff Henry Plummer, who was secretly the head of a network of over a hundred road agents, horse thieves, and murderers he had deputized. A mob of miners' vigilantes led by J. X. Beidler lynched Plummer and seven of his gang, while other vigilante groups hanged another twenty-six. The rest fled the gold fields.

"Our vigilance committee is not a mob," insisted the editor of the Montana *Post*. "Until justice can be reached through the ordinary channels, our citizens will be fully protected against these evil desperadoes, even if the sun of every morning should rise upon the morbid picture of a malefactor dangling in the air."

In the days before the Civil War, it was often difficult to tell who was the law and who was the lawless.

6

Mobs and the Black American: 1800-1863

MANY OF THE riots in America before and during the Civil War were over racial issues that increasingly polarized the nation. White southerners lived in fear of slave uprisings the way people lived at the foot of an active volcano.

In 1811 a slave named Charles led five hundred slaves in a revolt at the André sugar plantation north of New Orleans. Wounding André and killing his son, they seized arms and advanced down the coast smashing property and looting as white residents fled before them.

In a battle with several hundred U.S. troops and militia, eighty-three slaves were killed. Sixteen were arrested, tried, and executed in New Orleans. Their heads were mounted on poles at intervals along the Mississippi River as a grim warning to all restless slaves.

Whites were equally capable of rioting against blacks. In the late 1820s both free blacks and southern white migrants flocked to the booming city of Cincinnati. The whites grew incensed at the freemen for harboring fugitive slaves. Organizing a mob, they raided the black district, burned homes, and killed residents indiscriminately. Half the city's black population—over a thousand men, women, and children—were driven across the border into Canada.

In August 1831 panic swept white southerners when they believed the whole slave population had risen. The riots began with a thirty-one-year-old Virginia slave, Nat Turner, who fasted, preached, read the Bible, heard voices when he walked behind his plough, and told his revelations to awestruck fellow slaves. He had heard "a loud noise in the heavens," and a spirit had appeared to reveal that he had been chosen by God to lead the slaves out of bondage.

He plotted with disciples for a swift and terrible massacre that would terrify whites into fleeing before them.

Turner and five other slaves murdered their sleeping master, his wife, and three children. Seizing guns and ammunition, they sped from plantation to plantation gathering recruits until they were a mob of seventy. In each house they burst into they assassinated all white occupants, seizing muskets, axes, scythes, swords, and clubs. "A general destruction of property and search for money and ammunition," Turner revealed later, "always succeeded the murders."

They also took horses, which some slaves rode ahead to surround the next house and prevent its occupants from escaping before the mob could reach it. In two days, over fifty-seven white men, women, and children were slain in a twenty-mile area. Word flashed around the countryside, then through all the South.

"The slaves are plotting! The Negroes have risen!"

Militia units, three companies of artillery, and detachments of men from two offshore warships joined forces to suppress the slave mob. They swept through Southampton County killing over a hundred blacks indiscrimanately in a vengeful massacre. A company of white militia scattered Turner's mob with superior firepower. Many rioters were captured and killed on the spot; some were decapitated.

Of nineteen who were tried and executed, Gov. John Floyd observed, "All died bravely, indicating no reluctance to lose their lives in such a cause." Nat Turner, captured after two months, was jailed in chains.

When Turner was found guilty and hanged, northern abolitionist William Lloyd Garrison argued that the real culprits were not Turner and his slave mob but the whole country, which had to share guilt for the oppression of the slaves. The rioters, Garrison said, were no guiltier than "the Greeks in destroying the Turks, or the Poles in exterminating the Russians, or our fathers in slaughtering the British."

Many southern states, frightened that the Turner riot was only the first phase of a brewing full-scale slave revolution, passed new repressive measures against blacks. A 10:00 P.M. curfew was enforced by white patrols. Because Nat Turner had been literate, an Alabama law forbade anyone to teach a black to read, write, or spell, under penalty of a $500 fine.

In 1833 Gov. Robert V. Hane warned the South Carolina assembly, "A state of military preparation must always be with us [to prevent] domestic insurrection." South Carolinians were convinced that all slave riots were the work of "abolitionist spies" in the South, egged on by Garrison and his inflammatory newspaper, *The Liberator.* The state assembly made circulation of any publication inciting to riot punishable by the death penalty. In 1835 a mob of angry Charleston citizens broke into the post office, seized packages of antislavery pamphlets in the mail, and burned them.

Southern wrath at the abolitionists was matched by many racially prejudiced white northerners. In July 1834 a furious New York City mob, worked up over penny journal editorials accusing abolitionists of favoring racial intermarriage, sacked the home of abolitionist leader Lewis Tappan, wrecked two antislavery churches, and set fire to ghetto homes.

A gang of Boston truckers threatened to tar and feather

Garrison, then kill him, if he did not abandon the struggle to abolish slavery. Ignoring the threat, he agreed to speak to the Boston Female Anti-Slavery Society on October 21, 1835. He arrived to find a rowdy mob milling about the building entrance. Pushing through the throng unrecognized, he went up three flights to the meeting hall.

Some mob members had already seated themselves among twenty women abolitionists. Worried for Garrison's safety, the women persuaded him to retire to their office next door until Mayor Theodore Lyman could disperse the mob. But the rioters outside, now numbering over a thousand, refused to listen to the mayor. Ripping down and smashing the society's sign, they shouted, "We must have Garrison! Out with him! Lynch him!"

Lyman persuaded the women to call off their meeting to avoid "a scene of bloodshed and confusion." Garrison escaped out a back window by dropping onto a roof shed, but was spotted by the mob. He was pursued into an upper story of a carpenter's shop and captured. The roaring crowd in the street yelled brutal suggestions. *Throw him out the window!*"

A rope was tied around his body and he was forced to climb down a ladder into the arms of the mob, which tore off his clothes. Putting the rope around his neck, the hooting rioters dragged him through the streets. Garrison stumbled along in the center of the human storm as men ran alongside taunting him and spitting in his face. Some indignant observers, fearing the mob meant to hang him, pressed the mayor to act.

As the mob reached City Hall, on Lyman's orders some burly truckers smashed through its ranks, tore Garrison free, and rushed him to the mayor's office. The mob howled in dismay.

In hastily borrowed clothing Garrison was whisked out a back entrance into a carriage, which was spotted by the rioters. Hanging onto the wheels, they forced open the doors, grabbed the horses, and tried to overturn the vehicle. Police rushed in to tear them off, and the horses flew at full gallop to the Everett Street jail, where Garrison agreed to spend a night behind bars in protective custody.

"I would rather have the peril and outrage through which I have passed," Garrison wrote proudly after his mobbing, "than such a reception as Lafayette received. . . . Give me brickbats in the cause of God, to wedges of gold in the cause of sin."

Another celebrated abolitionist was less lucky—the youthful Rev. Elijah P. Lovejoy, who edited an anti-slavery journal in Alton, Illinois. By 1836 mobs had already attacked and wrecked his office, throwing his printing press in the river, three times. When the Ohio Anti-Slavery Society sent him a fourth press, Lovejoy was determined that no mob should touch it. Fifty young abolitionists agreed to help him guard it when it was delivered at night to an Alton store.

A large, drunken mob bearing torches attacked the store. In an exchange of gunfire, a rioter was killed. Roaring its fury, the mob put up a ladder and tried to set the roof ablaze. Lovejoy and some abolitionists rushed out of the store firing at the incendiary. Wounded, he toppled off the ladder.

A volley of shots rang out from the mob. Hit five times, Lovejoy was killed. When the hopelessly outnumbered abolitionists sought to surrender, the mob drove them back into the building and set it afire, shooting them as they ran out. Three were wounded, but the others escaped. The mob then broke into the burning store and destroyed the fourth press.

Passing decades increased the turbulence. In the Kansas Territory of the 1850s, pro- and antislavery mobs fought a bitter guerrilla war that cost the lives of two hundred men.

Abolitionist John Brown had little patience with eastern leaders of the antislavery movement. "These men are all talk," he fretted. "What is needed is action, action!"

In October 1859 he led eighteen men—five of them blacks—in a raid on the town of Harper's Ferry, Virginia. His purpose: to seize the arsenal, arm fifteen hundred local slaves, then lead them south along the Appalachians, freeing slaves as they went. They managed to capture the arsenal and take sixty leading citizens hostage, but were attacked by townspeople and forced to take cover in the engine house.

Marines led by Col. Robert E. Lee reinforced the town's defenders. A fierce gun battle left a dozen of Brown's followers dead, including two of his sons; one marine and five local citizens were also killed. Brown was clubbed into submission and brought to trial in a case that created a national sensation.

"Had I so interfered in behalf of the rich, the powerful . . . it would have been all right," Brown told the Court bitterly, "and every man in this court would have deemed it an act more worthy of reward than punishment."

On the day he was sentenced to hang, church bells tolled in mourning throughout New England and in Ohio and Illinois. "John Brown may be a lunatic," said the *Boston Post*, "but if so then one-fourth of the people of Massachusetts are madmen."

When the Civil War broke out in April 1861, many whites in northern and border states angrily blamed blacks in their midst. As law enforcement officials looked the other way, white mobs attacked black communities in Memphis, Louisville, Cincinnati, and Detroit.

The Enrollment Act, which made every northern adult male subject to military draft unless he could pay $300 to hire a substitute in his place, was fiercely resented by poor workingmen. Americans of Irish descent, who made up a fourth of New York City's 814,000 population, saw it as the kind of oppression their ancestors had suffered at the hands of British aristocrats. They were also furious at being forced to wage a "rich man's war but a poor man's fight" on behalf of blacks, who were being used as strikebreakers against their waterfront unions.

On the day the draft began, Monday, July 13, 1863, thousands of New York workers did not report to their jobs. Mobs armed with clubs, knives, and other weapons gathered on the streets and began converging on draft headquarters. Factories and workshops emptied as additional thousands, including women, joined their ranks.

The mood of the mobs grew uglier as they swelled in size. Telegraph poles were pulled down to disrupt communications. Reaching draft headquarters, rioters began hurling rocks. Windows were smashed. Sweeping some police aside, the vanguard surged against the doors and burst them open.

Shouting and yelling, they swarmed over the building, smashing furniture and chasing draft officials. The lottery wheel was splintered, all records were torn up and scattered. Setting the building on fire, the jubilant multitude cheered as flames crackled into the sky. Ringleaders caught sight of Police Superintendent John A. Kennedy hurrying to the scene.

"There's Kennedy—get him!" The mob closed in. Blows rained down, knocking him into a vacant lot. Fleeing, he was set upon by a second mob that caught him near a wide mud hole. *"Drown him! Drown him!"* A heavy blow with a club sent the chief of New York's police headlong into the water, where he was trampled and kicked savagely before he could escape.

A cry went against Horace Greeley's *Tribune*, champion of the abolitionist cause. *"Burn it! Kill Greeley!"* The mob raced to the *Tribune* building and hurled rocks at its windows, then burst into the printshop, wrecking everything within reach. Police charged into the mob, nightsticks flailing. When a flying squad of army troops arrived with a howitzer, bombs, and rifles, Greeley was horrified.

"Take 'em away!" he cried. "I don't want to kill anybody. Besides, they're a damn sight more likely to go off and kill *us!*" The mob was driven off without army help.

As night fell the rioters began hunting scapegoats they blamed for their grievances—black Americans. The first one seized was severely beaten, then hanged to a tree. Frightened blacks sought refuge in police stations.

Meanwhile the flames consuming draft headquarters spread to other buildings, as a mob of fifty thousand watched and cheered. Ringleaders clamored for the burning of every factory that employed blacks. A small body of troops fired a warning volley over their heads. Infuriated toughs fell upon the soldiers, snatching their muskets and clubbing them into flight. Some troops were beaten senseless and left for dead.

Police squads counterattacked, only to find themselves drowning in bodies as iron bars, clubs, and bricks smashed against their faces. Those police who could escaped, battered and bleeding. Some who were knocked unconscious or killed were stripped and robbed. One officer was chased by a mob led by a woman wielding a shoemaker's knife.

Fire companies seeking to fight the blazing buildings were driven off until a fire chief assured mob ringleaders that draft headquarters had been totally destroyed, and pointed out that some of the burning buildings belonged to leading Democrats who were "friends of the people."

Tuesday morning, July 14, dawned on a city stupefied by shock. Stores and factories stayed closed as an early mob of ten thousand poured into the streets. A force of police led by Sgt. Daniel Carpenter and seven hundred troops led by a Colonel O'Brien marched to break the mob up. At their approach many rioters ran to the rooftops, hurling down rocks and brickbats. Carpenter sent fifty police after them. One clubbed rioter fell off the roof, a four-flight plunge to his death. Others were beaten insensible, dragged downstairs, and thrown in the street. Troops brought up two, howitzers and trained them on the shouting masses. Bawling defiance, the mob charged. The howitzers fired point-blank; soldiers' muskets roared.

Men and women fell, shrieking in agony. One woman was killed with a baby in her arms. The mob scattered in panic.

Other mobs roamed the city seeking revenge for the morning's shootings. Police and rioters fought savagely, filling the pavements and gutters with bleeding and dying men.

Wall Street firms shut down and formed volunteer companies to serve under the military. Clanging firebells told of new buildings going up in flames. Shouts and cries from every direction signaled heavy street fighting.

Blacks continued to be hunted down savagely—"as hounds would chase a fox," Maj. Edward Sanford wired Secretary of War Henry Stanton. When one mob killed a black, it stripped him and did a triumphant Indian war dance around his body. Blacks who dared venture on the streets were chased to the river, and to save their lives had to dive in. Hundreds of blacks sought shelter at police precincts.

Toward evening reinforced troop and police forces took the offensive. One huge mob began throwing up street barricades made by lashing cars and wagons together. Four such barricades were erected in depth. As soldiers opened fire, police braved a hail of flying rocks and brickbats to tear down the barricades.

The mob fell back behind each rear barricade in turn.
Intense troop fire at last forced it to flee in wild disorder,
leaving behind forty dead and wounded.

On the third day of the riot, Wednesday, July 15, an
armed mob battled troops and forced them to retreat, leaving dead and wounded soldiers behind. Another mob seized
the Manhattan Gas Company, threatening to plunge New
York into darkness that night. The city was spared that
panic when fresh troops sent in from outside the city retook
the plant.

Black bodies were now hanging from lamp posts all over
the city. Troops attempting to cut them down were
attacked. Officers ordered canister and grapeshot fired
point-blank into charging mobs. Often five or six rounds
had to be fired before rioters were driven off. Street battles
raged in every quarter of the city. Houses and stores
continued to be gutted and looted, then sent up in flames.
Governor Seymour finally declared the city to be in a state
of insurrection.

By the fourth day, Thursday, July 16, Lincoln withdrew
Union troops from Gettysburg, only one week after the
crucial battle there, and sent them to New York. Losses and
defeats on the battlefield could be remedied, but to let New
York be reduced to a ruin of ashes might compel the war to
end. Loss of the great banking houses and financial
institutions would paralyze the government by cutting off
home funds and foreign credit. And a defeated draft in New
York would end the draft in every northern city.

Mayor George Opdyke called on citizens to form street
patrols to protect their districts from roaming gangs of
plunderers. Hoping to divide the ranks of rioters, he
announced that the draft had been suspended for the time
being, and that $300 exemption money would be paid to
any poor citizen who might be drafted, to pay for a substitute if he chose.

These concessions might have prevented the riots in the

first place, but by this time mob passions had soared too high and too much blood had been spilled. Knots of men filled the streets angrily vowing bitter vengeance against the military and police for "warfare against the people."

One large mob assaulted a platoon of soldiers, forcing them to take refuge in a foundry. Troop reinforcements rescued them by routing the rioters with fixed bayonets. The mob took out its fury by smashing and looting stores in every direction. Pursued, hundreds of rioters raced up to rooftops from which they poured down a murderous musket fire.

Troops rushed up with howitzers, sweeping the streets with canister. Eleven of the mob's ringleaders were killed; wounded bodies lay thick on the pavement. The troops then stormed the buildings and fought pitched battles in narrow halls and on staircases and roofs. Many rioters fought desperately until they were killed. Survivors fled.

Union troops from Gettysburg planted cannon on streets of the most turbulent sections, finally restoring an uneasy peace on the fifth day of the turbulence.

The riots had caused more deaths in those five days of anarchy than all that would occur in all the riots all over the nation a century later during the violent 1960s.

There were at least fifteen hundred known dead, with the actual figure higher because of many clandestine burials and an undetermined number of lynch victims thrown into the river. Uncounted thousands were wounded. Over three thousand blacks were left homeless. One out of five black New Yorkers chose to move to more law-abiding cities. Following the riot, not a single black showed up for work on New York's docks.

The holocaust of New York's Draft Riot, echoed by similar but less bloody riots in Newark, Jersey City, Troy, Boston, Toledo, and Evansville, forced change in the draft laws to eliminate discrimination against the poor. And the riots marked the beginning of an Irish-American solidarity that was to win them greater representation in politics and on the police force.

If the rioting in New York shocked Americans, it was no worse than official violence being committed by uniformed mobs on both sides of the Civil War.

"If we hang prisoners," said Col. John S. Mosby, leader of Confederate guerrilla forces, "it is simply in retaliation for similar treatment of our men. I hanged eight men on the Valley Pike yesterday in retaliation for those of mine executed at Front Royal."

In the fall of 1864 poet Walt Whitman, serving as a medical aide with the Union army, witnessed rioting by both Mosby's men and Union regulars, when the Confederates attacked a train full of wounded Yankee troops:

"No sooner had our men surrender'd, the rebels instantly commenced robbing the train and murdering their prisoners, even the wounded. . . . Two were dragg'd out on the ground on their backs, and were now surrounded by the guerrillas, a demoniac crowd, each member of which was stabbing them in different parts of their bodies. . . . The wounded had all been dragg'd (to give a better chance also for plunder) out of their wagons; some had been effectually dispatch'd. . . . Others, not yet dead, but horribly mutilated, were moaning and groaning."

Then a U.S. cavalry charge overwhelmed Mosby's men, and seventeen prisoners were taken. The Union soldiers ordered them to "make a run for it." When the rebels did, they were cut down by gunfire from all sides.

Uniforms did not make mobs any more respectable.

7

The Klansmen Ride

AT THE CLOSE of the Civil War, the white ruling class in the South sought to retain power by barring blacks from voting and by passing black codes to keep former slaves in peonage. "We hold this to be a Government of the White People," decreed the Democrats of Louisiana, "made and to be perpetuated for the exclusive political benefit of the White Race."

But the "carpetbaggers" (migrants from the North) and "scalawags" (southern anti-Democrats) in the Republican party were determined to outlaw black codes, strip ex-Confederates of their vote, and give it instead to black freedmen.

On the sultry afternoon of July 30, 1866, Radical Republicans assembled at the Mechanics Institute Hall in New Orleans to take over the Louisiana government, in the name of the Union, as part of Reconstruction. Supporting them, a crowd of black men came marching jubilantly down Canal Street to a small brass band headed by a flag-bearer.

A sullen white mob had gathered in the baking streets. When a white newsboy ran alongside the black marchers,

In 1866 a procession of freedmen marching to the Mechanics Institute Hall in New Orleans was attacked by a white mob. (*Culver Pictures*)

jeering and taunting, one marcher lost his temper and fired a horse pistol in the air to frighten him off. That was the spark police and the white mob had been waiting for. Police opened fire on the marchers while a mob of over two thousand charged the procession, driving it off with bricks and stones.

A second white mob attacked the hall, firing shots at Radicals watching the riot from windows. The Radicals fell to the floor as bullets shattered glass over them. Rioters led by police burst into the hall, firing wildly at the figures lying on the floor. Black Radicals leaped out the smashed windows, only to be shot down or stabbed by police outside.

"Police came up to Negroes and white men, indiscriminately taking no prisoners, but shooting them as rapidly as possible," State Senator J. D. O'Connell testified later at a congressional hearing. "I saw one policeman, while a Negro was kneeling before him and begging for mercy, shoot into his side. I saw another discharge his revolver into a Negro lying flat on the floor. . . . I saw a line of police [outside] . . . fire their revolvers into the hall."

By the time federal troops arrived to restore order, thirty-four blacks and four whites had been killed, and over two hundred people had been injured. Gen. Phil Sheridan reported, "It was not just a riot but an absolute massacre by the police . . . a murder which the mayor and police perpetrated without the shadow of necessity."

That riot sounded the keynote for southern defiance of northerners who treated the South as conquered territory. White southern mobs began terrorizing freed blacks and their white Radical Republican allies. General Sheridan revealed that during the bloody Reconstruction years, 1865 to 1877, over thirty-five hundred blacks and northern whites were killed or wounded in Louisiana alone.

The Radicals fought back by organizing mixed black and white militias to defend the freedmen and patrol elections. Their most important foe was the Ku Klux Klan.

The Klan was first organized in Pulaski, Tennessee, in 1866 as a white fraternal order. Its sinister possibilities were quickly recognized by a celebrated ex-general of the Confederacy, Nathan B. Forrest, when he was elected Grand Wizard. He began using it as an instrument for reversing what he felt to be an intolerable control of the southern social structure by former slaves and northern enemies.

Employing threats and mob violence to achieve its ends, the Klan united masses of white southerners behind its crusade, especially lower-class workers who feared the competition of free black labor.

Their success as terrorists inspired imitators like Louisiana's Knights of White Camela, Tennessee's Pale

Faces, North Carolinas Invisible Empire, and South Carolina's Invisible Circle.

In a typical tactic to frighten uneducated blacks, a mob of hooded Klansmen would knock on the door of a poor freedman's shack to demand a bucket of water. One would pretend to quaff the whole bucket while pouring its contents into a sack inside his robe. Patting his stomach, he would declare, "That's the first drink I've had since I was killed at Shiloh!"

Blacks were threatened, flogged, or tortured into staying away from the polls, and into giving up their political organizations. Those who resisted were murdered.

Carpetbaggers who risked excursions into the countryside away from the protection of federal troops were beaten, driven out of the state, or assassinated. "Unpatriotic" scalawags who dared oppose the Klan were hounded out of the South by ostracism, arson, and physical attacks. But first and foremost the targets of Klan terrorism were blacks.

Klan mobs usually drank heavily as they galloped about the countryside searching for victims. Carrying whips, pistols, and ropes, they lashed and tortured captives, killing anyone who tried to stop them. They frequently set fire to black schools and drove off black teachers.

By 1871 the terror spread by Klan mobs was so great that President Ulysses S. Grant issued a proclamation ordering Klansmen in South Carolina and Kentucky to "disperse within twenty days." He asked for an extra session of Congress to deal with the problem. Kentucky blacks petitioned the Congress for federal action against the Klan, which was "robbing whipping ravishing and killing our people without provocation, compelling Colored people to brake the ice and bathe in the Chilly waters of the Kentucky River."

Congress responded by passing the Enforcement Act of

1871. Grant urged southern whites to give it full support, pointing out that federal enforcement of the Fourteenth Amendment would not be necessary if local communities enforced it themselves.

But white supremacy forces of the South were determined to reimpose racist rule south of the Mason-Dixon line. In September 1874 the *Atlanta News* ran an editorial appealing to southern whites for a new wave of vigilante action:

"Let there be White Leagues formed in every town, village and hamlet of the South, and let us organize for the great struggle which seems inevitable. . . . We have submitted long enough to indignities, and it is time to meet brute-force with brute-force. . . . Act the moment Grant signs the civil-rights bill . . . a declaration of war against the southern whites. It is our duty to ourselves . . . to the white race."

White Leagues sprang up throughout the South. In Louisiana one mob of White Leaguers attempted to drive out the Radical Republican state government. A pitched battle with federal troops in the streets of New Orleans left over twenty dead and a hundred wounded.

Three months later a similar struggle for power took place in Vicksburg, Mississippi, where a white mob seized a black Republican sheriff and forced him to resign at gunpoint. When 125 blacks sought to reinstate him, they were stopped by a mob of armed white men. After a parley the blacks agreed to leave. As they retreated, the mob fired at their backs, killing 9 and arresting 20. The mayor covered up the massacre by telegraphing the Associated Press that Vicksburg was imperilled by "insurrection."

White mobs from Louisiana and Texas flooded into the city to fight blacks and "raise a little hell." Vicksburg soon seethed with ruffians who established mob law, breaking into homes, bullying citizens, and murdering twenty-nine blacks.

President Grant expressed disgust at the atrocities committed by the racist mobs. He urged southern governors to punish mob leaders, and instructed federal military commanders in the South to use their forces to prevent riots.

The northern press, meanwhile, preferred to run sensational stories about the misgovernment and corruption of black politicians in some southern states.

Rutherford Hayes, campaigning for president in 1876, was convinced that Reconstruction was a failure, and that Federal military intervention in the South was a mistake. White southern leaders assured him that if northern troops were withdrawn, blacks in the South would enjoy far greater personal safety, as well as protection of their civil rights.

Hayes preferred to believe it since he needed southern support to win his tight presidential race against Samuel J. Tilden. A contested election went to Hayes through fraud committed by three southern canvassing boards. Hayes soon began withdrawing federal troops from the South as a "much needed measure for the restitution of local self-government and the promotion of national harmony."

With black voters no longer protected by federal bayonets, one southern legislature after another was swiftly recaptured by white racists. Blacks were kept in subjection not only by Jim Crow laws but also by restoring prewar traditions enforced by lynch mobs. Lynched blacks were often charged with assaulting white women, but their true offense was generally expressing their opinions openly or engaging in political activity.

The final collapse of Reconstruction in the South was marked by a race riot in Wilmington, North Carolina, where Radical Republicans had managed to cling to office until 1898. On election eve a thousand "Red Shirts" held a rally to proclaim that they would "no longer be ruled, and will never again be ruled, by men of African origin."

"Go to the polls tomorrow," urged Democratic leader Alfred Waddell, "and if you find the Negro out voting, tell him to leave the polls and if he refuses, kill him, shoot him down in his tracks." Next day the Red Shirts ranged through the city with guns, menacing blacks who tried to vote.

The Democrats won easily. Two days later Red Shirts wrecked a black newspaper plant, then sent it up in flames. Surging through Wilmington's ghetto, pistols in hand, the mob shot every black in sight, killing almost a hundred. The Republican mayor and all black officials were driven out of office at gunpoint.

Texans fretted, however, because a black regiment continued to be stationed at a federal fort on the outskirts of Brownsville. To impugn the troops and force their removal, in 1906 a midnight mob of white Texans shot up the town, using stolen army ammunition and leaving the shells strewn around as evidence. One white citizen was killed by accident.

Fourteen white "witnesses" then swore they had seen a mob of black troops rioting in town. Herbert J. Browne, a detective hired by the War Department, questioned black private Boyd Conyers and reported that Conyers had confessed to having been the leader of the rioters. But upon the outbreak of the shooting, the post commander had ordered a roll call of the black regiment and had found all men present save two on pass. And an inspection had shown all their rifles to be clean.

Nevertheless, President Theodore Roosevelt decided that at least some of the accused had to be guilty and were being protected by the others. He discharged all 160 soldiers dishonorably, even though 6 had won the Medal of Honor and

13 had been cited for bravery in the Spanish-American War. The order cost the men their pensions and other rights and cast them into civilian life with bleak job prospects.

Sen. Joseph Foraker of Ohio accused Roosevelt, who had made racist remarks, of rank prejudice. Accusing the white witnesses of perjury, he offered impressive evidence that the black troops had been framed. President Jacob Schurman of Cornell University wrote Foraker, "I am absolutely convinced that the President has made a terrible mistake."

Roosevelt defended his decision by citing the detective Browne's report. But Sheriff E. C. Arnold, in whose presence Private Conyers had been questioned, then declared, "We kept Conyers under most severe cross-examination, but . . . he positively denied that he knew anything to tell. . . . The report of Mr. Herbert J. Browne . . . is the most absolutely false . . . perversion of what really did take place that I have ever seen. . . . I was both shocked and horrified when I read it."

It took sixty-seven years for justice to be done. In 1973 the Defense Department finally acknowledged to Conyers, last-known survivor of the Brownsville incident, that he had been discharged unfairly by Roosevelt. His discharge was changed to honorable, and he received a $25,000 indemnity.

It was too late to do anything about the 159 others.

8

Rioting on the Range and Picket Line

THE LATTER HALF of the nineteenth century and the early years of the twentieth were a stormy time of agrarian and industrial unrest marked by mob action, both against the law and in the name of the law. Many western pioneers felt that only vigilantism could preserve law and order in their distant settlements, which often attracted the lawless precisely because of the absence of effective courts and police forces.

To give the mobs they organized a semblance of legality, pioneers called them vigilance committees, committees of safety, and other high-sounding names. But in central Texas frontiersmen bluntly called them what they were—mobs.

Feuding sheepmen and cattlemen kept the range steeped in violence. In Wyoming four masked mobs of cattlemen attacked four sheep camps simultaneously. Blindfolding the sheepmen and tying them to trees, they clubbed to death eight thousand head of sheep. In Arizona the feud between Graham family cattlemen and Tewksbury sheepmen raged for five years, driving out peaceful ranchers and strewing the range with twenty-six dead cattlemen and six dead sheepmen.

In the last two decades of the nineteenth century, over two thousand lynchings were reported in the West and South, apart from thousands that went unreported. The number far exceeded legal executions. When vigilantes of Casper, Wyoming, hanged a man in 1902, they left this note pinned to his body: "Process of law is a little slow, so this is the road you'll have to go. Murderers and thieves, Beware! PEOPLE'S VERDICT."

"Lynching," wrote James E. Cutler in his book *Lynch-Law* (1905), "is a criminal practice which is peculiar to the United States." And in a society which stressed gallantry toward women, known victims of nineteenth-century lynch mobs included ninety-two females—seventy-six black, sixteen white.

With the federal government committed to a campaign of suppression and genocide against the red man, white mobs in the West felt free to raid Indian camps at will, killing and plundering. Little better than armed mobs were many western cavalry units glorified in the eastern press.

On November 28, 1864, Col. J. M. Chivington led a mob of militia from Fort Lyon, Colorado, against a camp of 500 peaceful Indians under Chief Black Kettle. Ignoring Black Kettle's raising of first an American flag, then a white flag, they attacked at dawn. Women and children, along with braves, were shot, knifed, mutilated, and scalped. Over 450 were left in various stages of dying.

A local newspaper reported enthusiastically that Chivington and his men had "covered themselves with glory" in the "Battle of Sand Creek." One year later Chivington was asked by congressional investigators why he had found it necessary to kill Indian children. "Nits make lice," he replied.

Indian agent John S. Smith testified, "I saw the bodies of those lying there cut all to pieces, worse mutilated than any I ever saw before; the women cut all to pieces."

81

Riot!

In 1890 the Seventh Cavalry under Col. James W. Forsyth surrounded a Sioux camp at Wounded Knee, South Dakota. Chief Big Foot offered to surrender, but Forsyth's men wheeled up cannon and trained them on the camp. All Indians were ordered to stack their arms. When one seemed slow in surrendering his gun, soldiers grabbed it from him.

It discharged accidentally. The shot excited the cavalry into a wild mob. They fired volleys point-blank into the Indian villagers. The artillery opened up, bombarding the center of the camp. Fleeing Indians were shot down. An estimated 250 Sioux men, women, and children were slain.

Gen. Nelson A. Miles, sickened by the massacre at Wounded Knee, relieved Forsyth of his command. But the War Department blamed the Indians and reinstated Forsyth, awarding eighteen Medals of Honor to his men. In 1973, eighty-seven years later, a group of young Sioux seized and held Wounded Knee to force the American people to recognize that their history books had not told the truth about the massacre, nor about many injustices done the Indian people.

In 1891 President Benjamin Harrison proudly told Congress, "Since March 4, 1889, about 23 million acres have been separated from Indian reservations and added to the public domain for the use of those who desire to secure free homes under our beneficent laws." And two years later Theodore Roosevelt observed, "It is nonsense to talk about our having driven most of these Indians out of their lands. They did not own the land at all in the white sense; they merely occupied it as the white buffalo hunter did."

One Indian chief said bitterly that the white man had made many promises to the Indians but had kept only one—the promise that he would take the Indian lands.

In the latter half of the nineteenth century the ethnic minority most often under attack by mobs continued to be the Irish, but Italian immigrants were also subject to popular hostility. Many were suspected of belonging to the criminal Black Hand, or Mafia, society. In March 1891, when New Orleans's chief of police was murdered, nineteen Italians were charged with the crime. A jury, however, found them innocent.

Angry lawyers, doctors, bankers, and merchants called a protest rally of six thousand citizens. "When the law is powerless," cried lawyer William Parkerson, "the rights delegated by the people are relegated back to the people, and they are justified in doing that which the courts have failed to do!"

He led an armed mob to the jail where the prisoners were still being held. Fifty men armed with Winchesters and shotguns smashed down a side door and broke into the jail. Prison officials made no attempt to stop the vigilantes as they murdered eleven of the Italians, shooting some in their cells and dragging others out to be lynched by the mob.

"Of course, it is not a courageous thing to attack a man who is not armed," Parkerson conceded later, "but we looked upon these as so many reptiles."

Southern intolerance was directed against three principal minority groups—blacks, Catholics, and Jews. Most mob actions had one of these three groups as targets.

One notorious riot involved Leo Frank, Jewish manager of a pencil factory at Marietta, Georgia. When fourteen-year-old Mary Phagan was found dead of assault and strangulation in the cellar of the factory in April 1913, she had managed to leave a scribbled note charging an unnamed black man with the crime. Factory worker Jim Conley was arrested. Turning state's evidence, he accused Frank as the killer.

On the day of Frank's trial, threatening mobs surrounded the courthouse. Notes were sent to court officials: "Hang the Jew, or we will hang you!" Judge and jury swiftly convicted Frank, who was not only Jewish but a transplanted northerner. The mob danced with joy in the streets, roaring its approval of a sentence of death by hanging. Conley, convicted only as an accessory, was sent to a chain gang for a year.

Georgia's governor, highly dubious of Frank's guilt, commuted his sentence to life imprisonment. An armed mob styling itself a "vigilance committee" drove in cars to the prison farm where he was held. The warden and guards offered no resistance as Frank was seized, driven off, and hanged.

Anti-Semite Thomas F. Watson, afterward elected to the U.S. Senate from Georgia, gloated in the newspaper he published, "A Vigilance Committee redeems Georgia and carries out the sentence of the law." The *Boston Traveler* spoke for a shocked North: "In this crowning demonstration of her inherent savagery, Georgia stands revealed before the world in her naked barbarian brutality."

Mob violence marked labor clashes of the late eighteenth and early nineteenth centuries. Sometimes the mobs were angry workers. Sometimes they were strikebreakers and private guards hired by antiunion corporations. Sometimes they were the police or troops who were turned loose to riot against workers.

"When their immediate interests were in question," noted sociologist Christopher Lasch, "the business classes had been ready enough to reply to violence with violence, indeed to instigate it. They were perfectly willing, if the need arose, to call out the federal troops to put down strikes and to recruit armies of Pinkerton detectives in the name of harmony and peace; and they were supported in these policies by respectable citizens everywhere. The middle class feared not violence so much as the threat to the *status quo.*"

This hostility to unskilled labor also reflected ethnic bigotry, since most business owners, foremen, and skilled workers belonged to native "old-stock" Protestant American families, while most unskilled workers were Irish, Slavic, German, Jewish, Italian, Hungarian, and other immigrant nationalities from southern and eastern Europe.

During the depression of 1873, unemployed New Yorkers planned a demonstration in Tompkins Square to demand public works programs. Police decided to refuse a permit, but did not notify labor organizers until the morning of the scheduled demonstration. By then over seven thousand immigrant workers and their families had jammed into the square on a frozen January morning. Among them was young Samuel Gompers, future leader of the American Federation of Labor.

He told of a sudden attack by mounted and foot police:

"Without a word of warning they swept down on the defenseless workers, striking down the standard-bearer and using their clubs right and left indiscriminately on the heads of all they could reach. Shortly afterwards the mounted police charged the crowd on Eighth Street, riding them down and attacking men, women and children without discrimination.

"It was an orgy of brutality. I was caught in the crowd on the street and barely saved my head from being cracked by jumping down a cellarway. The attacks of the police kept up all day long—wherever the police saw a group of poorly dressed persons standing or moving together."

Police Commissioner Abram Duryee, insisting that this violence had been necessary to suppress "communism," denied that the police had rioted like a mob. "It was the most glorious sight I ever saw the way the police broke and drove the crowd," he boasted. "Their order was perfect as they charged with their clubs uplifted."

Police of the day were regarded by liberals, radicals, and

the poor as the "cossacks of big business," in the pay of politicians who were in the pay of the corporations. In 1874 *Harper's Weekly* ran a caricature of police on its cover, showing them arresting women demonstrators against unemployment and high prices, while ignoring important crimes. The police were all drawn with the heads of pigs—anticipating by a century the epithet used against them by college students and black militants.

West Coast police looked the other way when mobs attacked another ethnic minority. By 1870 there were fifty thousand Chinese in California, most of them employed by the railroads on cheap labor gangs. White workers blamed them for depressing wages for the rest of labor. In 1871 a white mob sealed off the Chinese quarter in Los Angeles and raced over its rooftops with axes and guns. Smashing holes in the roofs, they fired shots and threw fireballs into the houses to drive out occupants. Some Chinese were dragged out and hanged in batches from awnings and wagon tops, among them a small boy. By day's end eighteen had been shot or lynched, and all Chinese stores looted.

Similar riots persisted in the West all through the 1870s. "The hoodlums need have no fear of punishment," *The New York Times* observed in 1874. "Of course, the municipal authorities . . . nominally object to the threatened riot, but inasmuch as the Chinese have no votes, while every hoodlum polls at least a score, no very vigorous interference with the popular will need be apprehended."

In 1875 coal miners in Rock Springs, Wyoming, struck for a pay raise. The company fired them and reopened the mines with 150 imported Chinese strikebreakers. A union mob stormed the Chinese quarter, shooting at every Chinese it encountered, and flinging torches into their lodgings. The massacre left 28 Chinese dead, 15 wounded.

A local grand jury refused to indict any white miners.

In 1877 a great railroad strike against slashed wages led to rioting and over ninety deaths in a dozen cities. In many cities strikers were peaceful until they were attacked by federal and state troops. After one clash in Reading, Pennsylvania, in which thirteen people were killed and forty-three wounded, a coroner's jury blamed the troops for an unjustified assault upon peaceful citizens.

In Pittsburgh troops advanced with fixed bayonets against a mob of thousands of workers, their wives and children, who threw stones at them. The troops opened fire, killing twenty people and wounding seventy. Enraged workers drove off the militia, burned down the depot, and destroyed over one hundred locomotives and two thousand railroad cars.

Even without the provocation of company-inspired attacks upon them, desperation drove many strikers to the use of violent tactics in the labor wars. They were forced to fight not only industry but its ally, the government.

Federal and state troops protected strikebreakers and thwarted strike strategy. Courts granted injunctions branding many strikes illegal. Strike leaders were often jailed or deported. Companies were allowed to lock strikers out of their jobs and blacklist them. "Yellow dog" contracts with company unions, specifying starvation wages, were held legal. When violence occurred, government officials talked darkly of "foreign agitators" and "anarchist conspirators."

The antilabor press echoed this line, and emphasized the corporation credo that the rights of private property were sacred. Even though a worker might have spent a quarter of a century at a job, he was not conceded to have any vested rights in that job. When it was taken from him and given to a strikebreaker, he often felt driven to fight for it tooth and nail.

Workers were particularly embittered when corporations, in periods of depression, kept up profits and stockholder dividends by slashing paychecks and firing employees.

In 1892 Carnegie steelworkers struck for that reason, shutting down the huge company plant at Homestead, Pennsylvania. General manager Henry Clay Frick prepared to reopen it with strikebreakers and hired three hundred Pinkertons to protect them.

When the Pinkertons sought to land from a river barge, they were met by a mob of several hundred grim strikers armed with Winchesters and pistols. A gun battle broke out on the river bank. Five men on each side were killed, and the Pinkertons were forced to surrender. The governor then ordered seven thousand troops to Homestead, enabling Frick to reopen the plant. Strike leaders were arrested, but not convicted by a jury that blamed the importation of Pinkertons.

"Workmen are strongly prejudiced against the so-called Pinkertons," observed the report of a U.S. Senate investigating committee, "and their presence at a strike serves to unduly inflame the passions of the strikers."

The violent Pullman strike of 1894 was called by U.S. Labor Commissioner Carroll D. Wright "probably the most expensive and far-reaching labor controversy . . . among the historic controversies of this generation." Arrayed against the strikers were the wealth of all the railroads, the power of the federal government, railroad-controlled courts, the press, the U.S. Army, and thousands of tough company police.

George Pullman's workers were outraged when he slashed their already low wages by 40 percent, at a time when his company was making large profits. Refusing to meet with the union's grievance committee, he declared arrogantly, "There is nothing to arbitrate." Three thousand workers went on strike. In sympathy the American Railway Union, led by Eugene Debs, refused to handle any trains carrying Pullman cars. The boycott paralyzed rail operations.

Railroad tycoons of twenty-four lines organized a General Managers' Association to crush the strike. Chicago police were ordered to break up workers' demonstrations. The GMA hired two thousand men who were made deputies by the U.S. marshal—men the Chicago chief of police himself called "thugs, thieves, and ex-convicts." Some were ordered to join the strikers as spies and agents provocateurs, to urge and provoke violence. They set fire to hundreds of cheap, worn-out freight cars, giving the antilabor press an opportunity to smear the strikers as a lawless mob terrorizing Chicago and to call for armed troops to shoot them down.

Not that the strikers themselves were wholly peaceful. To keep trains from running, many derailed freight cars, obstructed tracks, threw switches, and pulled scab engineers off trains. U.S. Attorney General Richard Olney, an ex-railroad lawyer and a railroad director, obtained an unprecedented federal court injunction against the blocking of trains, on grounds that the mails were being held up.

Over the protest of Gov. John B. Altgeld, President Grover Cleveland sent federal troops to Chicago. When Debs refused to call off the strike, cavalrymen and infantrymen with fixed bayonets charged a mass of strikers, killing twenty. Debs was arrested and sent to jail for six months.

The strike collapsed. Theodore Roosevelt praised Cleveland's method of suppressing the strike. The way to handle radicals, he declared, was to take "ten or a dozen leaders out, standing . . . them up against a wall and shooting them dead."

If mob violence was good enough for the bosses and government officials, decided tough labor leader Bill Haywood, then it ought to be good enough for workers. He

89

organized the radical Industrial Workers of the World, known as the IWW or Wobblies, to fight unscrupulous industrialists with terror and dynamite.

They matched the violence of Pinkertons and troops with counterviolence in copper mines, lumber camps, industrial plants, on waterfronts, and in agricultural areas. "Brigands on one side," said *The Nation*, "were faced by bandits on the other." But the only rioters who were arrested were those who belonged to the ranks of labor.

Perhaps the worst industrial riot occurred in 1913–1914 when ten thousand Colorado miners struck for union recognition. The companies imported mobs of armed thugs who were deputized by the local sheriff to give them legal powers. When the deputies evicted strikers from company homes, the workers took their families to tent colonies set up at Ludlow on land rented by their union. Mobs of deputies raided the tent colonies, and men were killed on both sides in gun battles.

To drive the strikers out of the mine fields, the companies sent deputies to attack them in an armored train called the Death Special. Miners ambushed it before it got to Ludlow, shot the engineer, and forced it to retreat.

Gov. Elias M. Ammons called out the National Guard. Assured it would protect them, strikers agreed to surrender over two thousand guns. But soon guardsmen were allowed to go home, their places taken by the deputized company thugs.

"By April 20 the Colorado National Guard no longer offered even a pretense of fairness or impartiality," reported George P. West of the U.S. Commission on Industrial Relations, "and its units in the field had degenerated into a force of professional gunmen and adventurers . . . subservient to the will of the coal operators. This force was dominated by an officer whose intense hatred for the strikers had been demonstrated." That officer was Lt. K. E. Linderfelt.

On April 20, 1914, he led his mob of guardsmen in an unprovoked attack on the Ludlow tent colony with rifles and a machine gun. Five men and a boy were killed, and the tents were set afire. Hundreds of miners and their families fled, pursued by flying bullets, but two women and eleven children were burned or suffocated to death in the tents.

"During the firing of the tents," West noted, "the militiamen became an uncontrolled mob and looted the tents of everything that appealed to their fancy or cupidity."

Three strike leaders were taken prisoner, then shot.

The mine fields erupted in a roar of hatred and rebellion against the authority of the state. Calling on all Colorado workers to arm themselves for revenge, mobs of furious miners attacked mine after mine, driving off or killing the guards, dynamiting and setting fire to buildings. In ten days of fighting another fifty-three persons were killed.

"This rebellion," reported West, "constituted perhaps one of the nearest approaches to civil war and revolution ever known in this country in connection with an industrial conflict." Federal troops finally restored order.

An appalled President Woodrow Wilson urged the Colorado mine owners to bring about industrial peace by recognizing the miners' union. Instead they pressed prosecutions of union leaders. One was convicted of murder, but the verdict was overturned by the state supreme court. None of the mine owners, Lieutenant Linderfelt, or any of their mobs were compelled to answer for the crimes of the Ludlow massacre.

The tragic record of violence in labor struggles of the late nineteenth and early twentieth centuries, with mobs rioting on both sides, brought little immediate benefit to American workers. Tens of thousands were either deported, jailed, injured, or killed, and many of their unions were destroyed.

91

Had the violence been only on the part of the workers, public opinion might have sided with the leaders of industry, who were supported by a captive press. But the violence unleashed by big business, through company thugs, police, national guardsmen, and federal troops, gradually sickened most Americans.

In the long run it made inevitable the public demand for industrial peace by legalizing labor's bargaining rights, on an equal basis with those of capital, in the 1930s. Only when that happened did the stormy class struggle subside and the threat of revolution disappear.

9

Mobs and World War I

THE ERUPTION OF World War I in Europe meant little at first to American workers, whose energies were absorbed in struggling for union recognition and decent wages.

June 1915 found striking workers angering Standard Oil by damaging company property at Bayonne, New Jersey. Armed guards, hidden behind piles of lumber, shot and killed 6 workers and wounded others. Sheriff E. F. Kincaid intervened, arresting 1 strike leader and 129 guards, of whom 10 were held for the grand jury. "I don't like the methods of wealth in employing gunmen and toughs to shoot defenseless men and women," the sheriff declared, "any more than I like the methods of strikers destroying property."

Under pressure, Standard Oil signed a one-year strike settlement. At the end of that time it provoked another strike and tried to operate with strikebreakers. When a police escort smashed through picket lines with scabs, a gun battle broke out, wounding four policemen and two strikebreakers. A mob of workers surrounded the police station next day, demanding an end to charges on their picket line.

Angry police responded by deputizing a mob of company

guards and rioting through the area where many strikers lived. Workers were clubbed, shot, and herded into their homes, and the saloons where they gathered were wrecked. Four were killed. Two weeks later the strike collapsed.

In 1916, as sentiment built up for America's entry into the war on the side of the Allies, there was a growing intolerance of antiwar labor militants as "Unpatriotic." Police broke up workers' meetings called by union organizers.

"One of the greatest sources of social unrest and bitterness," reported the U.S. Commission on Industrial Relations in 1916, "has been the attitude of the police toward public speaking . . . by persons connected with organizations of which the police, or those from whom they receive their orders, did not approve. In many instances such interference has been carried out with a degree of brutality which would be incredible if it were not vouched for by reliable witnesses. Bloody riots frequently have accompanied such interference, and large numbers of persons have been arrested for acts of which they were innocent."

In New York City, Police Commissioner Woods testified before the commission that upon taking over his office, he had found radical street meetings being rigidly suppressed in violation of the Bill of Rights, provoking frequent riots and bitter resentment of the police.

In the Northwest the IWW fought doggedly for free speech as indispensable in its campaign to organize Washington lumber workers. Each time IWW leaders sought to hold street meetings in Everett, they were beaten with clubs and run out of town by the sheriff and his deputies. Organizing a mob of over three hundred armed Wobblies, they sailed back in steamers.

At the landing they ran into a hail of dumdum bullets from the sheriff's mob of two hundred vigilantes. In a ten-minute gun battle for free speech, five Wobblies were killed and thirty-one wounded, while two vigilantes died with nineteen wounded. Only Wobblies were arrested, and seventy-four were put on trial for first-degree murder.

"The sheriffs in many counties deputize guards in the employment and pay of corporations, without any qualifications and sometimes without even knowing their names," reported the Commission on Industrial Relations. "Similarly, the militia are at times recruited from the guards and other employees of corporations. The private guards, detectives and vigilantes can have no other purpose in connection with a strike than to break it [by going] to unbelievable lengths."

The commission noted that the corporations had no difficulty in getting courts to issue blanket injunctions against strikers. "The subserviency of the courts in many parts of the country cannot be more clearly shown than by the fact that they have time and again permitted the militia, under color of so-called martial law, to usurp their functions."

When Woodrow Wilson declared war in 1917, he was particularly concerned about the spirit of violence it might unleash among the American people. "The spirit of ruthless brutality will enter the very fiber of our national life," he warned, "infecting Congress, the courts, the policeman on the beat, the man in the streets." His prophecy was quickly fulfilled.

In an atmosphere charged with suspicion and bigotry, criticism of the government became equated with disloyalty. Vigilante mobs sprang up all over the country to persecute as "un-American" all who dared challenge the status quo.

When pacifist minister Herbert Bigelow tried to address a meeting in Newport, Kentucky, a mob seized, bound, and gagged him. Driven into a forest, he was lashed unconscious with a blacksnake whip. The U.S. attorney general's office refused to investigate because charges had not been brought by a "responsible citizen."

Much later George Creel, head of the President's Committee on Public Information, admitted, "The sweep of mean intolerance, of course, developed a mob spirit. . . .The press, from which we had the right to expect help, failed us miserably."

Vigilante mobs smeared yellow paint on the houses of pacifists, raided schools to tear up German-language textbooks, forced dissenters to kiss the flag in public, and attacked radical labor meetings. A superpatriot mob known as the National Security League even accused three hundred members of Congress of disloyalty and forced an investigation.

"Several thousand private persons," said Attorney General Thomas W. Gregory, "most of them as members of patriotic bodies, [are] keeping an eye on disloyal individuals, and making report of disloyal utterances."

Gregory organized his own private intelligence-gathering organization, the American Protective League (APL), described by John P. Roche in his book, *The Quest For the Dream*, as "a government-sponsored lynch mob." The APL's two hundred thousand operatives secretly collected "intelligence" on labor "subversives" provided by bank presidents, railroad executives, corporation lawyers, and other captains of industry.

The war effort put enormous pressure on American workers. In some cases workers were compelled to stay on the job twelve hours a day, seven days a week, for low wages that remained frozen while businessmen were allowed to prosper on soaring prices. When unions struck, employers cried that Bolsheviks were spurring revolution. Vigilante mobs punished strikers by beatings, kidnappings, lynchings, and mass deportation out of town, county, and state.

In Bisbee, Arizona, a mob of two thousand businessmen and mining officials, organizing as a "Loyalty League," had themselves made deputies by Sheriff Harry Wheeler. In July 1917 these vigilantes rounded up 1,284 IWW strikers and sympathizers, then forced them into a cattle train provided by the railroad. The doors were sealed and the boxcars hauled into the blazing New Mexico desert, where the deportees were dumped and left to their own resources without food or water.

Compelled to act, President Wilson sent federal troops to their rescue. Sheriff Wheeler and 224 leading businessmen were indicted for illegal kidnapping and violation of civil rights, but not one of the mob was convicted.

In Oklahoma poor IWW tenant farmers and sharecroppers staged a "green corn rebellion," living on unripe corn while preparing to march on Washington to protest the war. Attacked by vigilante mobs, over 450 farmers were arrested by Oklahoma Home Guards for "conspiracy to oppose the draft." Leaders were sentenced to jail for ten years.

As war hysteria soared, Congress passed a Sedition Act in May 1918 to outlaw all criticism of the government, armed forces, Constitution, flag, and war. By war's end ultrapatriotic mobs had seized 1,260 dissenters, deporting 1,109 from their homes, tarring and feathering 64, kidnapping and whipping 55, forcing 23 to kiss the flag in public, covering 5 with yellow paint, and lynching 4.

Sanity did not return with the end of the war. Many Americans felt threatened by the example of a new revolutionary government that had arisen in Russia. Anti-Socialist feelings were intensified when thirty-six bombs were found in the post office addressed to Attorney General A. Mitchell Palmer and other government officials. A mob of servicemen tore in a May Day parade in Boston, killing one marcher and wounding several. New York rioters wrecked the office of the Socialist *Call*.

The worst May Day riots occurred in Cleveland, where

the APL, now reorganized as the Loyal American League (LAL), led a mob in attacking a parade of 35,000 workers. A platoon of mounted police rode into the marchers, clubbing down men and women. Army trucks and tanks, police cars and patrol wagons also knocked down and rode over fleeing workers. The riot left 1 man dead, 40 injured, 196 paraders in jai'.

Postwar rising prices and unemployment caused labor unions to wage intensive organizing campaigns. The big corporations resisted as usual with lockouts, strikebreakers, and armed thugs given badges as "deputies." But now they also called upon the government to smash all strikes as "Bolshevist."

The IWW opened a union hall in Centralia, Washington, to organize lumber workers. On Armistice Day, 1919, a mob of American Legion veterans attacked the hall. Smashing windows and breaking down the door, they ran riot through the building, destroying everything. Besieged Wobblies opened fire, killing four of their assailants.

Seizing IWW leader Wesley Everest, legionnaires beat and kicked him, smashing in his face with rifle butts. Arrest gave him only a temporary respite; that night a mob broke into the Centralia jail and dragged him out. "Tell the boys I died for my class," he called out to other IWW prisoners. The mob drove him to a bridge, hanged him from a girder, riddled his body with bullets, then threw him in the river.

Attorney General Palmer decided to make a mass round-up of known and suspected radicals. Appointing his protégé J. Edgar Hoover to head a new unit that became the FBI, he ordered simultaneous raids on their homes and offices in thirty-three cities all over the United States. On New Year's Day, 1920, the G-men arrested over six thousand people.

In Boston a mob of five hundred "Intelligence operatives" burst into meeting halls, lining up everyone for search, and illegally arresting six hundred persons for interrogation. In

Lynn, Massachusetts, thirty-nine people meeting to organize a co-op store were handcuffed, chained, and hauled off to prison.

The New Republic labeled Palmer's raiders a "governmental mob" engaged in a "colossal conspiracy against constitutional rights."

Many caught up in the Palmer raids were non-Marxist immigrant workers with no knowledge of their rights under the Constitution. In Detroit eight hundred people were held incommunicado for days in a filthy, windowless jail corridor with one toilet and no sinks, without charges being pressed against them. Most had to be freed for lack of evidence of any kind.

Severely criticized, Palmer defended his actions by insisting, "The government was in jeopardy. My private information removed all doubt." His information proved to be a farfetched "subversives" list of sixty thousand Americans whose views ranged from mildly liberal to radical.

A committee of distinguished lawyers headed by professors Felix Frankfurter and Zechariah Chafee of Harvard Law School branded the government's use of deputized mobs illegal. Federal Judge George W. Anderson agreed, stopping all government deportation of "undesirables." By that time 249 radicals had already been put on board ships bound for Russia.

The lynch spirit whipped up by Palmer did not fade away easily. When civil liberties lawyer Arthur Garfield Hays sought in 1921 to speak on the coal fields of Pennsylvania in defense of workers' rights, he was attacked by a mob in the pay of mining companies. Police stood by while they beat him up, then arrested Hays for "disturbing the peace."

Militant unionists were now just as ready to riot in self-defense as the government and industry were to use violence against them. When soft-coal miners called a national strike in 1922, mine owner William Lester fired all his workers in Herrin, Illinois. He replaced them with fifty strikebreakers hired through a Chicago agency, which also supplied armed guards. An angry mob of workers with guns attacked the reopened mine, firing until the scabs surrendered.

"I had no idea what I was running into," strikebreaker Joseph O'Rourke later testified. "I don't blame the miners much for attacking us, for we were unknowingly being used as dupes to keep them from their jobs. We were given arms when we arrived, and a machine gun was set up at one corner of the mine. Guards were with us all the time . . . tough fellows sent by a Chicago detective agency."

The strikers murdered nineteen of the scabs they captured. "They tied five men with me," O'Rourke related, "took us out on the road and told us to run. We ran and hundreds of bullets followed us. We staggered on, but finally three of our group fell, pulling the others with us, tied down, several bullet holes being in me already. I laid there while men came up and fired more shots into us from three or four feet."

None of the miners was indicted for murder, however, because a coroner's jury blamed mine owner Lester for having imported strikebreakers and armed thugs into Herrin, a move he knew was bound to provoke a bloody riot.

The scales of justice were much more often weighted against militant unionists. Most police in the 1920s were intensely antilabor, reflecting the views of department chiefs, judges, and politicians who were beholden to big businessmen for their appointment or election. They rarely arrested company mob leaders or deputies who beat, shot, and killed labor organizers, radicals, and strikers. On the few occasions they did, the company men were invariably acquitted.

10

Race Riots: 1918–1927

WORLD WAR I and its aftermath brought outbreaks of race riots as large numbers of black field hands migrated to the cities, especially in the North. Many were hired as strike-breakers but often had no real understanding of the issues. They merely saw an opportunity to escape miserable lives as sharecroppers.

In East St. Louis when unionized whites struck an aluminum plant in the summer of 1918, black strikebreak-ers were hired in their place. Loss of the strike precipitated one of the bloodiest race riots in American history. Angry white mobs raided the city's ghetto, driving through at top speed and shooting into black homes.

Blacks organized an armed vigilante mob to keep out all whites attempting to enter their district. When two white policemen in a squad car refused to leave, the mob opened fire, killing one officer and mortally wounding the other.

Police rioted, attacking every black in sight. They were joined by a white mob of three thousand crying for vengeance. Blacks were pulled from streetcars, stoned, clubbed, kicked, and shot. Black homes were set ablaze, and men, women, and children fired on as they ran out.

When National Guard troops were called out, they stood by encouraging the riot.

"I saw the mob robbing the homes of Negroes and then set fire to them," testified one victim, Beatrice Deshong, twenty-six. "The soldiers stood with folded arms and looked on as the houses burned. . . . The police and the soldiers were assisting the mob to kill Negroes and to destroy their homes. I saw the mob hang a colored man to a telegraph pole and riddle him with bullets. . . . They were as vile as they could be."

The death toll stood at fifty-seven known dead, with hundreds injured. Many stunned blacks fled back to the farms and small towns they had come from; others moved across the river to St. Louis.

A congressional investigation held the commander of the troops responsible, noting that they had "fraternized with the mob, joked with them and made no serious effort to restrain them." The police were also blamed because "they shared the lust of the mob for Negro blood. . . . Instead of being guardians of the peace they became part of the mob . . . adding to the terrifying scenes of rapine and slaughter."

But all charges against the police were dropped in an arranged deal whereby three officers agreed to plead guilty of rioting, and were fined a token fifty dollars each, paid for by the force. Only four white rioters were indicted for the murder of forty-eight blacks, while eleven blacks were charged with homicide in the deaths of nine whites.

The draft was traumatic for many northern blacks sent to training camps in the South. Black troops stationed at Camp Logan in Texas resented Houston police Jim Crow laws.

In the summer of 1918 a black army MP remonstrated with two white policemen who were rough in arresting a black woman for using abusive language to them. Pistol-whipped over the head four times, the MP was shoved into a patrol wagon with the woman. When another black MP sought to find out what had happened, he, too, was beaten up and jailed.

The news infuriated black troops at Camp Logan, and they broke into an ammunition storage room. Defying orders of their officers to disband, they marched on the police station in downtown Houston with loaded rifles. A countermob of off-duty police, national guardsmen, and armed civilians formed hastily.

"Lynch them!" cried the vigilantes, racing to a confrontation. Street battles flamed all night. By the time National Guard units were able to enforce martial law, a dozen whites were dead and fourteen wounded. The blacks suffered five casualties, one of them fatal. All those arrested were black.

Texas congressmen demanded that all black troops be withdrawn from the state. Four days later Secretary of War Newton Baker ordered that no more black draftees should be called up by the army. When the arrested black troops in Houston went on trial, sixty-five were sentenced to jail, some for life.

After the war ended, over twenty-six serious race riots broke out in different parts of the country. Returning white veterans in the North were angry at the shortage of available homes and jobs, blaming the large wartime migration of southern blacks to their cities and towns. In the South returning black veterans, who had been treated as equals by the British and French, refused to conform to "Uncle Tom" rules expected of them. In the first year after the war, seventy blacks were lynched.

Racial tension was high in Chicago, where fifty-eight black homes were bombed during and just after the war. Blacks were demanding an end to segregated recreational areas. In July 1919 a major riot developed when some black bathers at the lakefront insisted upon entering the water from a public beach used until then only by whites.

Black and white mobs brawling on the sand touched off a week of citywide rioting. Gangs of tough young whites from ward athletic clubs attacked blacks on the streets with guns and knives. Armed black mobs counterattacked. White adults in cars sped through black districts firing wildly, while black snipers fired back at them from concealment.

On the third day of the riots, white servicemen joined a civilian mob in driving blacks from their homes, which were then looted, wrecked, and burned. Some blacks were beaten unconscious and thrown into the flames. In reprisal, a black mob burned forty-nine houses in the white immigrant neighborhood west of the stockyards, leaving 948 people homeless.

The senseless riots claimed 38 lives—23 black, 15 white—and injured 537 persons. Order was finally restored by three regiments of state militia.

Illinois Attorney General Hoyne accused the Chicago police of flagrant prejudice for arresting mostly blacks, while promptly releasing the few whites apprehended. Gov. Frank Lowden appointed a Chicago Commission on Race Relations to investigate all causes contributing to the race riot.

The commission found blame on all sides. The city was faulted for segregated housing. Police and courts were found to dispense different justice to blacks and whites. White athletic clubs were condemned as breeding grounds for hoodlum mobs. Unions were blamed for keeping blacks out, employers for hiring blacks as strikebreakers or cheap nonunion labor, and blacks for accepting such jobs. For many blacks, however, the only other choices were welfare rolls or robbery.

A race riot broke out in September in Elaine, Arkansas, after black field hands refused to pick a cotton crop for starvation wages. Outraged white planters ordered the sheriff to "get those damn Bolsheviks." When he deputized a mob of vigilantes and raided Elaine, a gun battle blazed in which seven blacks and two whites were killed.

The posse arrested ninety-two blacks, of whom a dozen received death sentences, the rest terms of twenty years to life imprisonment. On appeal, the U.S. Supreme Court set all the defendants free because the state of Arkansas had sought to deprive them of life and liberty without due process of law, merely imposing harsh sentences under "mob domination."

Responsibility for much of the racial warfare could be traced to a resurgence of the Ku Klux Klan, which rose again to oppose new black demands for equality spurred by the war. The Klan quickly grew so powerful that many eminent southerners felt compelled to join, particularly politicians. For a while the Klan dominated the state governments of Texas and Oklahoma, and stiffened all Jim Crow codes in the South.

At its peak the revived Klan claimed five million members. Its targets were not only blacks but also Catholics, Jews, foreigners, labor leaders, atheists, and others whose views offended Klan members. In 1921 alone Klan mobs deported forty-three victims, tarred and feathered twenty-seven, flogged forty-two, kidnapped five, killed four, and mutilated two. Klansmen rarely felt the hand of the law.

Defiance of the Klan was a risky matter in the Deep South. In Texas the Klan used elaborate spy systems and surveillance squads to ferret out opponents for punishment. Phones were tapped, telegraph messages intercepted, spies stationed in post offices. One of the braver Texans was the father of Lyndon B. Johnson, Sam Ealy Johnson, who cast one of the few votes in the state legislature for an anti-Klan resolution.

In 1926 Hiram W. Evans, Imperial Wizard of the Klan, explained candidly why Klansmen took mob action against those who were not white, Protestant, "God-fearing" native Americans:"We are afraid of competition with peoples who would destroy our standard of living."

Mob violence by the KKK grew so arrogant and brutal that national revulsion finally set in. Important figures began resigning with open denunciations of the Klan as a vicious organization, and courts fought free of its powerful influence in perverting justice.

"There can be but one governing authority," challenged Judge A. E. Gamble of Alabama. "One system is the courts of our State, the other is a body of masked men, responsible to no one, exercising their own power, crushing the weak without excuse."

What brought the Klan down, finally, was the corruption of its leaders. Klan officials were convicted of looting the organization's treasury, while the Grand Dragon went to prison for assaulting and murdering a young girl. Klan membership went downhill.

Ironically, when a thousand robed and hooded Klansmen marched in a 1927 Memorial Day parade in Jamaica, New York, they were set upon and beaten up by an outraged mob of New Yorkers. This taste of their own medicine deeply offended Klansmen, who considered that they alone had the franchise for mob violence.

11

Mobs in the Depression

A MOB OF five hundred jobless, hungry men and women gathered at City Hall to listen to Floyd Phillips of the Oklahoma City Unemployed Council denounce the economic system that denied them work and refused them emergency relief. The date was January 20, 1931. Passions aroused, they rushed after Phillips into a nearby grocery store to seize food for themselves and their families. Store manager H. A. Shaw tried to reason with them.

"It is too late to bargain with us!" Phillips shouted.

A police emergency squad rushed to the scene, lobbing tear gas shells into the mob. Gasping and weeping, crushed rioters smashed store windows to escape. Police arrested five women and twenty-six men, charging Phillips with inciting a riot.

Mobs of unemployed were making similar raids on food stores in cities across the country. The Great Depression was under way. In Chicago over 40 percent of workers were jobless, and a third of the city's million people were in desperate circumstances. In the summer of 1931, over two hundred poor families a week were evicted on court orders for being unable to pay their rent. Mobs of angry sympathizers gathered ominously when men, women, and children were dumped out of their homes with no place to go.

In August when the furniture of Mrs. Diana Gross, a seventy-two-year-old Chicago black woman, had been put on the street, an outraged mob of five thousand black and white people defied police and bailiffs by carrying it back inside her flat. Three of the mob were arrested, and one policemen fired a warning shot.

At that the agitated mob fell upon the police and beat them severely. The police drew their guns, killing three rioters and wounding a number of others.

When twenty thousand whites and forty thousand blacks marched in a mass funeral for the dead men, there was grim talk of the need for an uprising. Nervous authorities quickly announced a temporary suspension of all evictions.

In Congress, New York's crusty Hamilton Fish, Jr., blamed the disorders on "half a million Communists" who were seeking to subvert the nation. His remedy was not jobs but deportation. A few thousand Communists were, indeed, agitating among poor workers and tenant farmers, but the unemployed needed little goading to organize and protest their plight.

In March 1932 some five thousand jobless auto workers in Detroit marched to the Ford plant in Dearborn to demonstrate against layoffs. When they resisted Dearborn police efforts to turn them back from the Ford gates, hand-to-hand fighting broke out. Ford firemen knocked down workers with high-speed water hoses, while the police hurled tear gas, then opened fire with a machine gun. Four workers were killed, a dozen badly wounded.

When thirty thousand sullen workers attended the funeral ceremony for the victims of the Dearborn massacre, the *Detroit Times* declared, "The killing of innocent workmen . . . is a blow directed at the very heart of American institutions."

Agriculture lay in a shambles. The Depression ruined farm prices, but taxes and mortgage obligations remained constant. Unable to meet taxes or bank payments, thousands of farmers lost their land. On a single day in April 1932, a quarter of the whole state of Mississippi went under the hammer of auctioneers. "Right here in Mississippi some people are about ready to lead a mob," growled Gov. Theodore Bilbo. "In fact, I'm getting a little pink myself!"

Grim-faced farmers organized armed mobs to keep each other's homesteads out of the hands of court officials and banks. Jamming into foreclosure auctions, they would threaten to shoot any outsider who tried to bid. Auctioneers would be forced to sell the property after two bids of $1.00 and $1.18, and it would be restored to its original owner.

"We will soon have no individually owned and operated farms," Milo Reno, leader of the Iowa Farmers' Union, warned his members. "We have come to the place where you must practice what every other group does—strike!"

In the summer of 1932 he organized a farm holiday to stop food shipments into Sioux City until farmers were paid at least their cost of production. Mobs of farmers armed with ax handles blocked all roads leading into Sioux City with logs and spiked telephone poles. Trucks that sought to crash through the blockade had their tires slashed with pitchforks, and their windshields and headlights smashed.

The farm strike spread swiftly throughout Iowa. The Milk Producers Association dumped gallons of milk in roadway ditches to dramatize the senselessness of a system that refused to pay farmers fair prices for their food, while hungry Americans swelled long breadlines in the cities.

The governor ordered all roads cleared. The first county

sheriff who tried to obey had his gun and badge taken away and flung into a corn field. Other sheriffs swore in carloads of deputies who attempted to break through the blockades with convoys of nonstriking trucks. But the mobs of farmers stood fast, guns raised and ready for battle. The trucks turned back.

The farm strike spread throughout the country. A farm holiday mob in Nebraska stopped a freight train headed for market, driving off a carload of cattle. The mob's leader warned, "If we don't get beneficial service from the legislature, two hundred thousand of us are coming to Lincoln and we'll tear that new state capitol building to pieces!"

To end the farm strike, Congress hastily passed the Agricultural Adjustment Act providing farm price supports, and the Farm Credit Act that promised to keep the sheriff and mortgage company away from the doors of debtor farmers. Only then did the farm holiday mobs break up, and the farmers return to their barns and fields.

In June 1932 thousands of jobless veterans flocked to Washington to demand immediate payment of a promised bonus. The Bonus Marchers, many accompanied by their wives and children, set up a large shanty town on the Anacostia Flats, just outside the capital, building shacks from packing cases and scrap lumber.

They lobbied Congress with the demand, "Give us our bonus—or give us jobs!" The House obliged with a bonus bill, but the Senate voted it down. Twenty thousand angry veterans vowed to stay in Washington until they got their cash or "until hell freezes over."

War Department officials feared that a veterans' riot might develop and touch off Communist-led uprisings in every major city. President Herbert Hoover nervously put the White House under guard, chained the gates, and ordered Gen. Douglas MacArthur to drive the veterans out.

Four troops of cavalry with drawn sabers led six tanks and a column of steel-helmeted infantry through downtown Washington. Unarmed veterans in the city fell back before fixed bayonets and barrages of tear gas. MacArthur's forces crossed the Anacostia Bridge after midnight and attacked the veterans' encampment. Cavalrymen with drawn swords ordered the immediate evacuation of frightened women who began to gather up their meager pots, pans, and family belongings.

Weeping wives and screaming children fled with their husbands through clouds of choking tear gas. Troops set fire to their shacks with torches. Cavalry horses frightened by the tumult reared out of control, endangering the fleeing civilians. Some furious veterans challenged riders to dismount and fight. One cavalry unit rode into a mob of veterans, bowling them over like tenpins. Veterans trying to drag a cavalry captain from his mount were driven off by bayonets.

The tear gas killed an eleven-month-old infant and partially blinded an eight-year-old child. A number of people were hospitalized with bayonet and saber wounds.

The national media reacted with stunned anger. Many editorials correctly predicted that Hoover had made a stupendous error of judgment that would doom any hopes he had of reelection.

The president desperately sought to cover up his blunder by labeling many of the Bonus Marchers Communists and criminals. MacArthur called them "a mob . . . animated by the essence of revolution."

Realizing these protestations had little credibility, the administration then denied that the troops had committed any acts of violence or fired the camp. Newsreels of the riot disproved these claims, too.

Wherever the president went after that, he was met by a storm of boos. In the November election he went down to a crushing defeat at the hands of a man who promised suffering Americans a "new deal"—Franklin Delano Roosevelt.

In the month before Roosevelt took office in March 1933, angry mobs were verging on insurrection. In Seattle, a mob of thousands seized the county building. In the Blue Ridge Mountains, hungry crowds smashed store windows and seized food. In Des Moines, groups of protesters boarded streetcars and told conductors to collect their fares from the mayor. In Chicago, a mob tore down a four-story building and carried it off brick by brick.

The new president's emergency measures on behalf of the unemployed and poor farmers brought a measure of peace. But in 1934 there was a new wave of discontent because relief payments were inadequate, jobs still scarce, and employers as intransigent as ever about recognizing unions.

In April a Minneapolis mob of six thousand fired stones, bottles, and lumps of coal through the windows of City Hall, demanding higher welfare payments or government-made jobs. The following month the city's teamsters went on strike for union recognition. Business leaders fought them with a deputized "citizens' army." A clash with twenty thousand teamsters left two men killed on either side, and sixty-seven truck drivers wounded. The violence ended only when the teamsters won union recognition.

Violent strikes were waged by streetcar workers in Milwaukee, cab drivers in Philadelphia and New York, and auto parts workers in Toledo, where an excited British correspondent cabled home, "Toledo is in the grip of civil war!"

If mobs of workers rioted in their fight for union recognition, their employers did not hesitate to use even greater violence against them. A chief target of badge-wearing mobs was the Southern Tenant Farmers' Union (STFU), organized by Socialist leader Norman Thomas, which united ten thousand black and white sharecroppers in eighty integrated locals.

In Arkansas the STFU had to fight armed mobs organized by planters, absentee corporations, landlords, plantation managers, deputies, and vigilantes. STFU meetings were broken up and members jailed on trumped-up charges. Evicted from land holdings, they were denied relief payments. Their homes were riddled by machine-gun fire, their churches burned. "Riding bosses" hunted down STFU organizers. Union members were flogged, shot, and murdered.

Forty states issued injunctions against organizing unions, striking, and picketing. Union men who tried to defend themselves and their headquarters against company-organized mobs were often jailed for assault with intent to murder. California's Imperial Valley was put under mob rule by sheriffs and deputies to prevent, by any means, the organization of thousands of miserably paid fruit workers.

In July 1935, however, the New Deal established a new climate of recognition for labor's rights. The Wagner-Connery National Labor Relations Act created a National Labor Relations Board (NLRB), with the power to compel employers to negotiate with unions elected by their employees to represent them. The Wagner Act gave tremendous impetus to unionization of the biggest industries in the country, a drive led by the CIO under John L. Lewis, leader of the mine workers.

The administration also recognized that most labor violence was provoked by company-hired mobs, not strikers. A committee of the House of Representatives reported, "There are in the United States individuals and organizations whose regular business is furnishing for large fees strong-arm men and thugs in almost any numbers. . . . These mercenaries are transported from State to State by their employers, who . . . furnish them with weapons of clubs, brass knuckles and firearms. Their entry on the scene of any labor dispute usually means bloodshed . . . death or injury to innocent people."

In June 1936 a mob of such company thugs attacked strikers in Kent, Ohio, with tear gas and buckshot, seriously wounding fourteen pickets. An outraged Congress passed a Strike Breaker Act making it a felony to transport anyone across state lines to obstruct or interfere with pickets.

When General Motors workers called a strike in December, employees in the Flint plant surprised the nation by an unusual tactic. Instead of walking out and setting up picket lines, they "sat down" in the plant, capturing it and holding it for six weeks. Flint police who tried to throw them out were driven off with volleys of nuts, bolts, pop bottles, steel hinges, metal pipes, and coffee mugs. After a three-hour skirmish in which no one was seriously hurt, the baffled police, under orders not to use their guns, retreated.

GM's management found itself equally baffled. Michigan Governor Frank Murphy refused to send troops to drive the sit-downers out, even when they seized other GM plants. Importing private guards and strikebreakers was now forbidden under the Strike Breaker Act. A new Walsh-Healey Act, moreover, denied government contracts to any corporation paying substandard wages. And the Wagner Act compelled employers to permit union elections and bargain with elected representatives.

GM fought back by obtaining a circuit-court edict ordering the strikers to evacuate the plants. But when Flint's sheriff sought to enforce it, thousands of steel, rubber, and auto unionists marched into Flint to defend the sit-downers.

After six weeks General Motors gave in, recognized the United Automobile Workers, and signed a labor contract with the union.

This bloodless capitulation led to the surrender of the big steel companies, then to the unionization of other giants like General Electric and Firestone. For the first time in American history, labor had been strengthened to relatively equal power with industry. Workers' vested interest in their jobs was now recognized as equal to corporations' vested interest in their plants and equipment.

Although U.S. Steel and other major steel firms accepted unionization, "Little Steel"—Bethlehem, Republic, Youngstown Sheet and Tube, and Inland—did not. Managed by hardline ultra-conservatives, Little Steel determined to slug it out with the union, laws or no laws. The Strike Breaker Act, moreover, could only prevent the importation of scabs and thugs across state lines, not those hired intrastate.

Republic Steel provoked a strike by refusing to recognize the steelworkers' union, and kept its South Chicago plant open with strikebreakers who slept inside the plant, protected by hired armed guards. Police on the payroll of the companies harassed picket lines, and Mayor Edward Kelly refused to allow more than sixteen pickets at each gate.

Defying this ban on Memorial Day, 1937, some three thousand strikers set up a mass picket line in front of Republic's gates. When they refused to disperse, three hundred uniformed company police hurled tear gas and fired point-blank into workers' ranks. As groaning strikers fell, guards charged over the dead and wounded to club and shoot down those who fled, continuing their violence into a street full of spectators.

"It was almost beyond description, Senator," testified eye-witness Darrell C. Smith later before Sen. Robert La Follette's investigating committee. "It was just about the bloodiest scene possible. . . . I saw women struck with those iron bars just as mercilessly as though they were men. I saw

Scores of strikers were injured and a number killed on May 30, 1937, as uniformed guards attacked the picket line at the Republic Steel plant in South Chicago. (*Wide World Photos*)

a group of school children across the street running around in panic, scared, crying at the top of their lungs because they were frightened out of their wits. . . . These guards were rushing around . . . beating the people to the brick pavement, and then beating them after they were down."

Another eye-witness, reporter Dwight L. Buchanan of the *Canton Repository*, testified, "Four company guards . . . directed their aim . . . into a crowd which had gathered in a restaurant. . . . In this crowd were fifteen children caught in the gunfire as they were returning from Burns school."

Ten strikers were killed, six shot in the back. Fifty-eight more demonstrators and spectators had been wounded. The guards reported sixteen injuries of their own.

Mayor Kelly's police chief rushed to the defense of the company, insisting that it had been necessary to open fire on a bloodthirsty armed mob led by "outside agitators" and "Communists." Not a single demonstrator was proved to have had a gun, but the Chicago press echoed Little Steel's charges.

The steelworkers, learning that Paramount Pictures had made a newsreel of the riot, demanded that the film be released. Paramount executives refused, claiming it might "incite local riot and perhaps riotous demonstrations." Senator La Follette subpoenaed the film for his committee, which was shocked by its scenes of company police violence.

"We think it plain that the force employed by the police," the committee reported, "was far in excess of that which the occasion required . . . a deliberate effort to intimidate the strikers." Little Steel was found to have had seven thousand guards, patrolmen, deputy sheriffs, national guardsmen, city police, and company police on its payroll for strike duty, spending over $4 million to crush the strike and using $141,000 worth of munitions in the process.

The exposure of the Memorial Day massacre marked the last gasp of die-hard industrialists to smash union labor, and soon after Little Steel was under union contract, too.

For black Americans the Depression was just one more cross to bear. In 1930 black leaders pointed out that in the past half century, over forty-five hundred of their people had been murdered by vigilante mobs. In Atlanta a group of indignant white women formed an Association of Southern Women for the Prevention of Lynching. They secured fifty thousand signatures to a pledge "to create a

117

new public opinion in the South which will not condone for any reason whatever acts of mobs or lynchers."

In March 1931 an Alabama mob tried to lynch nine black youths, the Scottsboro Boys, who were charged with assaulting two white girls who had ridden a freight train with them. But authorities in Scottsboro sought to uphold the law, while satisfying the mob with what Lincoln Steffens called a "new-style lynching."

The nine youths were given a quick trial and sentenced to death on the flimsiest evidence. National protest, however, forced a commutation of their sentences to life imprisonment. When one of the girls confessed to the falseness of the charges, a long court battle finally compelled the release of all nine youths.

But lynchings continued. In the first year of the New Deal, twenty-four blacks were lynched. In Tennessee a twenty-fifth victim was saved by troops sent by the governor, whereupon the frustrated mob burned down the courthouse.

When the Justice Department began prosecuting lynch mobs under an old 1866 civil rights law, many southern states got the message and began taking steps to prevent mob violence.

In a northern race riot in 1935, for a change blacks rioted instead of being rioted against. When a black youth in Harlem was caught stealing a penknife in a five-and-ten, he was taken to the basement by a policeman who gave him a stern lecture and let him go through a rear entrance. When he did not reappear, a black shopper shrieked that he was being beaten by police in the basement.

A mob of shoppers formed, demanding to be shown the boy. Arriving police pressed them to the exits. At this a riot broke out and the store was forced to shut down. A rumor swiftly spread through Harlem that a black boy had been murdered by police in the basement of the five-and-ten.

Huge mobs gathered around angry street speakers who called for "wiping out" whites in a race war. When the police attacked the speakers, an excited mob of ten thousand blacks surged through Harlem smashing into, looting, and gutting two hundred white-owned stores. All night long the streets resounded to the crash of windows, screaming sirens, and firing of shots.

Many blacks fought hand-to-hand battles with the police, who killed three rioters and wounded thirty others. Over two hundred blacks and whites were treated for injuries, and over one hundred blacks were arrested. Damage to property: $2 million.

Police hunted for "criminal elements" responsible for the riot. But when Mayor Fiorello La Guardia ordered an investigation, his commission found its underlying causes to be the black community's anger over discrimination, unemployment, and police brutality. Unless these conditions changed, the commission warned, more riots could be expected.

La Guardia considered the commission's report inflammatory and refused to release it. But the black newspaper *Amsterdam News* managed to secure a copy and published it.

In 1940 Ralph Bunche, then a professor at Howard University, agreed to cooperate with Swedish sociologist Gunnar Myrdal on a study of prejudice in the United States. Bunche wrote him, "There are Negroes . . . who, fed up with frustration of their life here, see no hope and express an angry desire 'to shoot their way out of it.' I have on many occasions heard Negroes exclaim, 'Just give us machine guns and we'll blow the lid off the whole damn business.' "

When Myrdal arrived in the United States, he and Bunche took a trip through the South, interrogating both whites and blacks on the race question. In one town they were pursued by a mob of white "rednecks" and barely escaped with their lives. Out of their investigation came Myrdal's classic work, *The American Dilemma*, which found that the underlying cause of racial violence was whites' fear that social equality for blacks would result in intermarriage.

12

Home Front Violence: World War II

ONE OF THE most bizarre mobs in American history took to the streets in 1938 as a result of national jitters inspired by Hitler's threats of world conquest. On Sunday, October 30, the twenty-three-year-old "boy genius" of the Mercury Theater radio program, Orson Welles, broadcast a highly realistic radio dramatization of H. G. Wells's science fiction thriller, *War of the Worlds*.

After the initial announcement, the CBS program pretended to be an hour of dance music, which was constantly being interrupted by news bulletins about a strange flaming object that had fallen on a New Jersey farm. Finally a breathless reporter described furry-bodied monsters with wet leathery faces and serpentine eyes emerging from a huge cylinder. He announced the arrival of state police, and then over terrible screams gasped that the monsters had destroyed them with jets of fire. The monsters were headed his way. . . .

Crashes. Silence. When CBS had "reestablished contact," another hysterical announcer reported that New Jersey was in the hands of Martians, who had already destroyed seven thousand national guardsmen. More cylinders were landing, and the highways were clogged with fleeing civilians. The "U.S. secretary of the interior" interrupted to appeal for national calm.

By this time wild panic was sweeping many parts of the United States. Listeners who had tuned in late were convinced that they were hearing real news flashes; others, incredibly, forgot the opening announcement. The greatest hysteria broke out in New Jersey and New York, where people felt they were in immediate danger from the "Martians."

Frightened callers jammed police switchboards seeking information on where it was safest to flee. Others phoned in eyewitness reports of battles between Martians and earthmen. Doctors everywhere had their hands full treating people for shock and hysteria. In Jersey City police had to plead with frantic mobs to get off the streets. In Orange, New Jersey, an excited motorist stampeded a theater by rushing in to shout that the state was being invaded. In Alabama and Virginia people gathered in the streets to pray for deliverance. In some Midwest cities wild mobs ran through the streets looting and rioting while women and children hid in the churches.

By morning radio broadcasts and newspapers had managed to calm down the nation with assurances that no Martians had invaded the earth. Most people who had panicked felt foolish. Some were furious, like the farmer who had thrown up a fort of sandbags, which he had manned all night with a shotgun and pitchfork.

Columnist Dorothy Thompson wryly suggested that Orson Welles be given a congressional medal for having "cast a brilliant and cruel light upon the failure of popular education."

The outbreak of World War II in Europe found American sentiment sharply divided. Millions wanted no part of another foreign war, and many favored Hitler's anti-Semitic and anti-Communist policies. Some police were hostile to American anti-Fascist demonstrators and beat them up in Boston, Bridgeport, Cambridge, and Jersey City.

In imitation of Hitler's Storm Troops, anti-Semite William Dudley Pelley organized a mob of paramilitary Silver Shirts. Father Charles Coughlin, editor of *Social Justice* and founder of the Christian Front, regularly broadcast Nazi hate propaganda in radio "sermons" to forty-five million listeners.

In New York City mobs of rowdy Christian Mobilizers roved the streets and subways to pick fights with Jews, assaulting them with weapons. Others infiltrated crowds listening to speakers in the open-air forum at Columbus Circle and sought to start anti-Semitic riots. In 1939, on orders of Mayor La Guardia, 233 Christian Fronters were arrested on charges of inciting violence.

"The hate-rousing and anti-Semitic activities" of the Christian Front, warned the nonsectarian magazine *Equality*, might "eventually culminate in a violent, bloody rioting such as the city has never known." The liberal Catholic *Commonweal* accused Father Coughlin of seeking to inflame Fascist-minded mobs into "street demonstrations, control of the gutters—bombs and rifles and setting up a dictator by force."

In Jersey City, New Jersey, political boss Mayor Frank Hague used mobs of ward thugs to break up anti-Fascist meetings. Speakers were thrown out of the city or arrested for "vagrancy" and held incommunicado for days. "As soon as they begin to shout about 'free speech' and 'free press' and 'civil rights,' " Hague declared, "I know they are Communists."

It was in Hague's bailiwick that the Ku Klux Klan held a joint rally with the pro-Nazi German-American Bund in

1940, burning a huge cross and singing Nazi marching songs.

In March 1941 a mob of Christian Mobilizer storm troops attacked an anti-Fascist street meeting in Manhattan, shouting, "We want Hitler!" Shoving two women off a speakers' platform, they sent spectators flying with fists and bludgeons. There were no arrests. An investigation by Mayor La Guardia revealed that 407 members of the New York City Police Department were members of the Christian Front, and many others were sympathizers.

The battle of Britain, however, swung American sentiment sharply against Nazi Germany and its American apologists. Intolerance began to rear its head on the other side, with angry mobs attacking all who opposed going to war against the Axis powers. One major target was Jehovah's Witnesses, the pacifist religious sect that considers it idolatry to salute the flag of any nation. In 1940 mobs in forty-four states made no less than 340 assaults on the Witnesses.

After Pearl Harbor the Fascist movement in the United States disintegrated rapidly. Father Coughlin's weekly, *Social Justice*, was banned as seditious, and twenty-eight anti-Semitic leaders were indicted by a grand jury. But the government was careful not to encourage a repetition of the illegal mob violence that had characterized World War I.

"There has been almost no interference by legal authorities or by mobs with public meetings," noted Socialist leader Norman Thomas in 1943. Roger Baldwin, director of the American Civil Liberties Union, added, "We experience no hysteria, no war-inspired mob violence, no organization of virtuous patriots seeking out seditious opinion, and no hostility to persons of German or Italian origin."

Baldwin did note, however, the forced evacuation by the government of Americans of Japanese origin from West

Coast homes to inland concentration camps. Earl Warren, then attorney general of California, defended the order as necessary to keep California mobs, outraged by Pearl Harbor, from "taking the law into their own hands." But in 1944 the Supreme Court ruled it illegal to detain any loyal American citizens in custody, regardless of their ethnic origin.

A boom in defense jobs gave employment to many Mexican-Americans in Los Angeles. Chicano teen-agers in the *barrios* (Mexican-American neighborhoods) exhibited their new prosperity by a new clothing style known as "zoot suits." Subjected to insults and attacks by Anglo servicemen and police, they organized groups to defend the *barrios*. The anti-Mexican Hearst press called them "zoot-suiters" as a pejorative code name for all young Mexican-Americans.

In June 1943 rumors spread through Los Angeles that zoot-suiters were assaulting female relatives of servicemen. At the same time rumors circulated in the *barrios* that sailors were molesting and insulting Mexican-American girls. Street brawls broke out between groups of servicemen and Chicanos.

The Los Angeles *Daily News* ran a blatantly inflammatory headline: "ZOOTERS PLANNING TO ATTACK MORE SERVICEMEN."

A mob of several thousand soldiers, sailors, and civilians raged through the streets of downtown Los Angeles, beating up every Chicano they could find. Breaking into theaters, they ordered house lights up, then dragged Chicanos out of their seats into the street, beating them savagely. Anyone wearing a zoot suit was pulled off streetcars, assaulted, his clothes shredded.

Police either stood by or arrested the victims. A one-legged Chicano who asked why he was being arrested was knocked down with three blows of a nightstick, kicked in the face, and thrown into a police wagon. A Mexican

Mobs of servicemen stopped streetcars in downtown Los Angeles looking for zoot-suiters. (*Wide World Photos*)

mother who protested the arrest of her fifteen-year-old son was hit across the jaw by a police club. The "zoot suit riot" ended only when the military put downtown Los Angeles out of bounds, clearing it of servicemen with MP's and shore patrols.

Another serious race riot occurred in Detroit two weeks later, this time between whites and blacks. Detroit was filled with southerners of both races who had migrated north for defense jobs. Cramped into slums, tents, and trailers, their tempers were at flash point. Racial friction in war plants was inflamed by the demagoguery of white supremacists like Father Coughlin and Gerald L. K. Smith.

On a Sunday evening in June 1943, a spate of rumors followed a brawl in Belle Isle amusement park between whites and blacks. Whites heard that rioting blacks had assaulted a white woman, and blacks heard that white sailors had thrown a black woman and her baby into the lake, while police beat up blacks. Neither rumor had the slightest basis in fact.

Shortly after midnight whites began attacking blacks as they emerged from all-night movies in downtown Detroit. In reprisal blacks pulled whites off buses driving through the city's ghetto and beat them up. Police rushed to the ghetto, using guns and nightsticks against black mobs, who began smashing the store windows of white merchants.

Cordoning off the black district, police patrolled it in squad cars. Jumping out with drawn revolvers and riot guns, they shot at anyone suspected of looting or burning a store. Some suspects, told to "run and don't look back," were shot in the back. Black spectators were clubbed.

Mobs of whites swept through the streets wielding iron pipes, clubs, rocks, and knives. Police made no attempt to stop their assaults on blacks, even in front of City Hall. Before federal troops were called in to bring Detroit's "Bloody Week" to an end, 25 blacks and 9 whites had been killed. Another 319 people had been injured, with 1,500 arrests and $2 million worth of property destroyed.

Analyzing the riot, the *Detroit News* observed, "Southern whites have come here in vast numbers, bringing with them their Jim Crow notions of the Negro. Southern Negroes have come here to take jobs which give them for the first time in the lives of many of them a decent wage, and a sense of freedom they have never known before. The embers smouldered a long time . . . a slight incident caused them to burst into flame."

Thurgood Marshall, later a Supreme Court justice, pointed out that Detroit's white police had "enforced the law with an unequal hand. They used 'persuasion' rather than firm action with white rioters, while against Negroes they used the ultimate in force: night sticks, revolvers, riot guns, submachine guns, and deer guns." Conceding that many blacks had been looting stores, he noted that whites had been burning cars and stabbing and beating blacks. Yet the police had killed seventeen blacks and no whites. "The entire record . . . reads like the story of the Nazi Gestapo."

13

Riots in the Cold War Era

THE COLD WAR that followed World War II, marking increasing hostility between the United States and the Soviet Union, brought a sharp rise of intolerance toward all Americans politically left of center. Liberals and Socialists were both denounced as "Reds." Manipulating mob fears, demagogues in Congress ran witch-hunt investigations to ferret out "Commie spies in government." President Harry S. Truman branded the new mob spirit "typical postwar hysteria."

The Korean War touched off widespread anxiety that the Russians might fire nuclear weapons at American targets. Residents of county seats and small towns debated what to do if mobs of urban dwellers fled the big cities to seek refuge in countryside bomb shelters. Some rural Americans urged forming vigilante groups to shoot down any who tried.

On a beautiful warm August evening in 1949, over three thousand New Yorkers drove upstate to Peekskill to hear an open-air concert featuring the world-famous black baritone Paul Robeson. The local paper had angrily protested that the artist was an avowed Communist, and that the concert's sponsor, the Civil Rights Congress, had Communist affiliations.

Local veterans' groups, trying but failing to get a court injunction to stop the concert, urged members to take matters into their own hands. As soon as the recital began, someone cut off the lights and a mob of veterans charged into the amphitheater. Swinging baseball bats, they drove out both artists and audience. The concert was rescheduled a week later.

This time Gov. Thomas E. Dewey agreed to send one thousand state troopers for protection. The recital took place, despite a police helicopter that kept swooping low over the audience in an obvious attempt to drown out the music.

As cars began leaving the site, drivers found all exit roads lined with mobs of veterans and local toughs armed with bats. When rioters attacked the cars, troopers and county police either stood by idly or joined in. Windshields and windows were smashed, cars stopped, and drivers dragged out.

A Brooklyn victim beaten up by veterans and police said, "They were wild, and swinging indiscriminately at everyone with their clubs . . . in the most violent and vicious manner I have ever experienced."

Veterans screamed unprintable remarks at the drivers, threatening, "You'll never get out of here alive!" Roads for miles around were littered with broken glass and bloody smears. When Governor Dewey ordered a grand jury investigation, a blue ribbon panel decided that the mob had acted "justly" out of resentment of communism.

In August 1950 several thousand opponents of the Korean War held a rally in New York City despite denial of a permit. "Some of the demonstrators who refused orders to disperse were badly beaten by the police," reported *The New York Times*. "Some were charged by mounted police who rode onto crowded sidewalks."

American Fascist groups used the Korean War as a

pretext for organizing the anti-Communist National Renaissance party (NRP). Distributing anti-Semitic and Fascist literature, its elite guard of storm troopers engaged in fist fights and brawls with Jews, liberals, and civil rights workers.

In 1963 the NRP held a "Mass Open-Air Rally to kick Pro-Reds and Race-Mixers out of Yorkville," New York City's German-American community. The rally drew four thousand sympathizers. When a mob of Jewish War Veterans attempted to break it up, they were beaten off by mounted police.

Later that same year a mob of NRP storm troopers attacked labor pickets in the Bronx. Eight leaders were arrested and convicted on thirty-two charges of riot, conspiracy, unlawful assembly, and illegal possession of firearms.

The end of World War II, like the end of previous wars, also saw the rise of new mob violence against blacks.

"Almost every victim of lynching since the war has been a veteran," observed John Gunther in *Inside U.S.A.* "The Negro community is . . .more aggressive in its demand for full citizenship—even in the South—than at any other time in history. Roughly one million Negroes entered the armed services. They . . . learned what their rights were; overseas, many were treated decently and democratically by whites for the first time in their lives; the consequent fermentations have been explosive."

This new black determination inevitably produced a powerful white backlash. In 1946 a white mob in Columbia, Tennessee, beat up James Stephenson, a young black veteran, for hitting a radio repairman who had slapped and kicked Stephenson's mother. Stephenson and his mother were then arrested and spirited out of town to prevent a lynching. The frustrated mob raced through

Columbia's black quarter, firing into homes. Blacks fired back from windows, wounding two policemen.

Next day state troopers and police cordoned off the ghetto, then attacked it. Shooting out store windows, they smashed showcases, gutted the premises, and robbed cash registers. Homes were broken into without search warrants, and twenty-seven blacks who possessed hunting rifles were arrested. Two were shot while being held in jail. The rest were finally released after an unsuccessful attempt to convict them of "plotting to stage an armed insurrection."

The Ku Klux Klan announced its revival at a March 1946 meeting in Atlanta. In July thirty Georgians stopped a car with two black couples and murdered them. In August a Louisiana mob kidnapped two young blacks, dragged them to the woods, beat them savagely, and killed one by burning him alive with a blowtorch. Local authorities made no arrests, finding "no clues in connection with the reputed mob action."

In December 1946 President Truman issued an Executive Order establishing a Committee on Civil Rights, which called for a federal law against lynching; integrated housing; denial of federal aid to any state practicing discrimination; and an end to all restrictions on black voting. When southern congressmen killed such legislation, Truman vowed to make it a campaign issue. "Dixiecrats" bolted the Democratic party.

After winning the 1948 elections, Truman set an example for the country the following June by ordering integration of all swimming pools in the nation's capital. A number of cities followed suit. Mississippi congressman John B. Williams wrathfully warned of "bloodshed and race riots."

Some white mobs fulfilled his prophecy. The worst occurred in St. Louis, where police permitted white youths to drive blacks out of the public pool at Fairground Park with baseball bats. Racists spread a false rumor that a black youth had stabbed a white boy to death. That night over five thousand furious whites milled through the park beating every black in sight.

Black demands for integrated housing made working-class whites in the North increasingly hostile. A five-day riot broke out in Chicago, sparked by fears engendered when a white labor official moved into all-white Peoria Street and held a union meeting in his house that included eight blacks.

The fear of blacks moving into a neighborhood was even more pronounced in Cicero, a Chicago suburb inhabited chiefly by working-class whites. In June 1951 Harvey Clark, Jr., a black war veteran, attempted to move his wife and two children into an all-white Cicero apartment building. The suburb's racist police force sought to prevent the move, but were ordered to stand aside by a court injunction. A howling mob whipped up by a White Circle League attacked the building the day after the Clarks moved in.

Their flat was looted and their furniture thrown into the street where the rioters set it afire. Police watched passively. When the Clarks still refused to leave, the mob returned next day to wreck the whole building.

Gov. Adlai E. Stevenson ordered in the National Guard. Cicero's town president, attorney, and police chief were indicted by a federal grand jury on charges of conspiracy and violation of civil rights. Many townspeople were indignant at the state for interfering in what they considered a "legitimate" expression of community feeling.

White racists in the South were infuriated by the Supreme Court decision of May 1954 ordering an end to public school segregation. This death knell for the separate education of whites and blacks clearly foretold federal integration of all public facilities. Leading southern busi-

133

ness and professional men, encouraged by Sen. James Eastland of Mississippi, organized White Citizens Councils to thwart integration.

The greatest racial violence was perpetrated by white mobs in Mississippi. In 1955 they murdered a black minister and two young blacks, including fourteen-year-old Emmett Till, who was accused of "whistling at a white girl." Mississippi juries quickly acquitted the murderers of all three.

In September 1957 a court order compelled the school board of Little Rock, Arkansas, to admit black children to Central High School. But when nine black teen-agers arrived at the school, they found entry blocked by national guardsmen sent by Gov. Orville Faubus to keep them out, and by a hostile mob of over a thousand white citizens.

Guardsmen crossed their bayonets grimly in front of little Elizabeth Eckford when she tried to pass. Retreating in fear, she was followed by a mob of white women shrieking, "Get a rope! Lynch her!" Dr. Benjamin Fine, education editor of *The New York Times*, put his arm around the girl to protect her.

"Let this child alone!" cried a college professor's wife, Mrs. Grace Lorch, to the mob. "Why are you tormenting her?" She hurried the weeping Elizabeth to safety aboard a passing bus. The frustrated mob turned on Dr. Fine. Instead of coming to Dr. Fine's defense, the guardsmen threatened to arrest him for "inciting to riot."

Next day Mayor Woodrow Mann wired the White House: "The immediate need for Federal troops is urgent. The mob is much larger in numbers at 8 A.M. than at any time yesterday. People are converging on the scene from all directions and engaging in fisticuffs and other acts of violence. Situation is out of control and police cannot disperse the mob."

Federal troops were needed to protect black students from white mob violence during the integration of Central High School in Little Rock, Arkansas, in 1957. (*Wide World Photos*)

Outraged, President Dwight Eisenhower rushed a thousand army paratroops to Little Rock, and took the guardsmen out of Faubus's control by federalizing them. Under the protection of federal forces, the nine black children won entrance into the school.

The troops had to stay in Little Rock for a whole year to keep the children safe from the mobs.

135

14

The Ghettos Explode

THE FIVE YEARS between 1963 and 1968 may have been the stormiest in American history except for the Revolutionary and Civil wars. Over two million Americans took to the streets in activities that resulted in over nine thousand casualties, two hundred deaths, and seventy thousand arrests. Over a million Americans marched in civil rights demonstrations, over seven hundred thousand in anti-Vietnam protests, and another two hundred thousand participated in urban riots.

Many Americans were upset by this turbulence and favored harsh "law and order" crackdowns to suppress peaceful crowds as well as violent mobs. They were also irked with the media for reporting riotous behavior by police or troops against peaceful demonstrators.

Gov. George Wallace of Alabama spoke for the "silent majority" when he assailed all militant civil rights and antiwar leaders as part of a sinister conspiracy to destroy American society. Actually, many of those leaders attempted to bring about constructive change peacefully. In contrast, the wild urban riots that erupted were spontaneous and unled.

A study of seventy-six race riots by sociologists Stanley Lieberson and Arnold R. Silverman found that most broke out in northern ghettos overcrowded by jobless blacks who had immigrated from the rural South. Rioters, in effect, pushed aside nonviolent black leaders who had failed to win social justice by negotiating with the white power structure.

Their spontaneous uprisings were not directed so much at white persons as against white-owned property and against oppressive guardians of that property—policemen, firemen, and national guardsmen. Lieberson and Silverman noted that cities with a fair number of black middle-class property owners and black councilmen, and an integrated police force, suffered the fewest number of riots.

Much of the violence that occurred during the stormy events of the 1960s, as described in the first chapter of this book, was not the work of rioting protesters, but of mobs that rioted against the protesters. Sometimes those mobs were made up of police and national guardsmen. In other cases law enforcers encouraged violent mobs to beat up demonstrators by turning their backs or arranging to be absent.

Jim Peck, one of the Freedom Riders attacked by southern mobs in 1961, said, "They put fifty stitches in my head and face to put me back together again. . . . When Police Chief Connor was asked why there was not a single policeman at the Birmingham Trailways terminal to avert mob violence, he explained that since it was Mother's Day, most of the police were off-duty visiting their mothers."

Black Power agitators like Stokely Carmichael and Rap Brown did encourage race rioting by insisting that a white campaign was under way to exterminate all blacks, and that it was necessary to fight back violently. But much less was heard by the public about far more numerous white racist agitators like Connie Lynch, a self-ordained preacher who had been a Klansman. Speaking in Florida just after a black church in Birmingham had been blown up, he declared: "If they can find those fellows [who did it] they ought to pin a medal on them."

The mob he exhorted roared wildly in approval.

Some of the worst riots took place in Birmingham during the spring of 1963. When four thousand black men, women, and children marched peacefully through the city singing, "We Shall Overcome," Eugene "Bull" Connor's police attacked them with clubs and shocked them with electric cattle prods. Firemen assaulted them with powerful fire hoses that knocked them down and swept them along the streets with such force that the streams stripped bark from trees and tore bricks from walls.

In the long hot summer of 1964, when southern mobs destroyed forty black churches and terrorized hundreds of civil rights workers, Floyd McKissick, national director of CORE, said grimly, "I'm committed to nonviolence, but I say what we need is to get us some black power!" Black rage began to explode in the North, at the point of least resistance.

A Harlem riot broke out when Thomas Gilligan, an off-duty white police lieutenant, shot a fifteen-year-old black schoolboy. A huge mob roared its approval as black leader Jesse Gray called for "one hundred dedicated men who are ready to die for Negro equality." For five days rioters raged through the ghetto, "trashing" white-owned shops and attacking police with bottles and other missiles. Police charged with nightsticks as racing blacks yelled, "Whitey, we gonna get you!"

"I saw a bloodbath," declared CORE leader James Farmer. "I saw with my own eyes violence, a bloody orgy of police . . . police charging into a grocery store and indiscriminately swinging clubs . . . police shooting into tenement windows and into the Theresa Hotel. . . . I saw bloodshed as never before. . . . People threw bottles and bricks. I'm not saying they were not partly to blame. But it is the duty of police to arrest, not indiscriminately shoot and beat."

The Harlem riot touched off others in Brooklyn, Rochester, Chicago, Philadelphia, and three cities in New Jersey.

Early in 1965 President Johnson promised Martin Luther King and other black leaders that he would press for a new omnibus civil rights bill if they would try to keep black protest channeled to peaceful demonstrations. In March King organized a nonviolent march through Alabama from Selma to Montgomery. The President was outraged by the violence they encountered. "The Alabama state troopers took matters into their own hands," Johnson accused. "With nightsticks, bullwhips, and billy clubs, they scattered the ranks of the marchers. More than fifty men and women were severely injured. The march was over."

A white mob assaulted three white clergymen from the North, shouting, "Hey, nigger lover!" Boston minister James Reeb was clubbed to death. Thousands of clergymen participated in an indignant sit-in at the White House to protest.

Defying Alabama's lawmen, a new assemblage of twenty thousand Freedom Marchers completed the march from Selma to Montgomery. That night one of them, Mrs. Viola Liuzzo, a white mother of five children, was shot dead by a white mob. President Johnson urged Congress to investigate the Klan.

The House Un-American Activities Committee found that the Klan had 381 klaverns (chapters) throughout the South and also in six northern states. Many members belonged to local police forces. All Klan mobs operated under oaths of secrecy enforced by "beatings, bombings and, yes, even death."

139

To counter Klan violence, Louisiana church deacon Charles Sims organized the Deacons for Defense and Justice. Black vigilantes in fifty chapters were pledged to use weapons in self-defense only. "Klansmen bring the fight to us," Sims declared. "We guard white and black civil rights workers from white terrorists' bullets, and churches from bombs."

The crisis year of 1967 marked the beginning of race riots on a frightening scale. President Johnson appointed the National Advisory Commission on Civil Orders to study the causes and patterns. The commission's findings, called the Kerner Report, gave the principal reasons, in order of importance, as: police brutality; idleness caused by unemployment; slum housing; unequal education; poor recreational facilities; inability to get grievances heard; white insults; prejudiced courts; government neglect of black problems; ghetto overcharging by white merchants; inadequate welfare programs.

"The urban disorders of the summer of 1967," said the report, "were not caused by, nor were they the consequence of, any organized plan or 'conspiracy.' " The typical black rioter was found to be not a hoodlum or criminal, but a young high school drop-out without a job or employed in a menial job. He was proud of his race, hostile toward both whites and middle-class blacks he considered Uncle Toms, and cynical about expecting any help from the political system.

The worst race riots of 1967 occurred in Newark and Detroit. Newark was seething that July because of black complaints against police brutality and because, in addition to twenty-four thousand unemployed black adults, twenty thousand jobless black teenagers had no place to go and nothing to do.

An angry mob quickly formed when white police were seen clubbing and kicking a black cab driver as they dragged him into a police station. A firebomb was thrown against the station wall, burst into flame, and was followed by a barrage of rocks. Police charged out, clubbing everyone in the mob within reach. That triggered a four-day riot of rock-hurling, firebombing, window-smashing, looting, and car-burning.

Newark's 1,300-man police force was reinforced by 475 state troopers and 4,000 national guardsmen. The streets echoed with persistent gunfire, most of it aimed at looters, with many wild bullets striking innocent people. Rumors of black snipers made the young, inexperienced guardsmen nervous and trigger-happy. When they mistook one of their own men for a sniper, they poured fire into a housing project.

A number of men, women, and children were killed. "You have now created a state of hysteria," Newark's police chief raged at the guardsmen. He later said in disgust, "Guardsmen were firing upon police and police were firing back at them."

State troopers shot at blacks standing on their own porches. Guardsmen shot into a passing car, killing a ten-year-old boy. An eleven-year-old boy whose mother sent him out with the garbage was shot and killed. Guardsmen and state troopers rode around in jeeps firing into stores with "Soul Brother" signs in the window. Some seized black youths, put pistols to their heads, forced them to say foul things about their race, then pulled the trigger on an empty chamber.

When the Newark riot finally ended, twenty-one blacks had been killed, including six women and two children, and over $10 million worth of property had been burned or looted.

The Detroit riot took place a few weeks later, sparked by a police raid on ghetto gambling clubs, during which eighty-two blacks were arrested. A mob began rioting in protest, then turned to hurling bricks through shopwindows and looting. Firebombs flew, and a high wind swept the flames through the city. Fire companies were driven off with stones.

Some black militants were disgusted by the looting. "I wanted to see the people really rise up in revolt," said one. "When I saw the first person coming out of a store with things in his arms, I really got sick to my stomach. . . . Rebellion against white suppressors is one thing, but one measly pair of shoes or some food ruins the whole concept."

Gov. George Romney proclaimed a state of emergency and rushed in national guardsmen. "These poor kids were scared," declared Police Commissioner Ray Girardin, "and they scared me." Spraying bullets wildly at real or imagined snipers, they killed many innocent people, as in Newark.

Some snipers did attack police, firemen, and guardsmen, whose Patton tanks rumbled through the streets with machine guns blazing, strafing buildings suspected of harboring snipers. National Guard Major Robert J. Lewis said, "We told the men before they moved in here that they're not fighting the Viet Cong—they're fighting their own neighbors." But one young guardsman declared grimly, "I'm gonna shoot anything that moves and is black."

Blacks suspected of being snipers were shot dead, then found to be unarmed. Many suspects were taken to police stations, beaten up to force confessions, then taken off to hospitals. Over seventy-two hundred people were arrested. Of forty-three persons killed in the riot, thirty-three were black.

Order was finally restored by a task force of federal paratroops with strict orders not to fire unless they could see the specific person they were aiming at. Indiscriminate mass fire at buildings, cars, or mobs was forbidden.

Flying over Detroit in a helicopter, Governor Romney

said, "It looked like the city had been bombed . . . with entire blocks in flames." Damage was estimated at $32 million.

"Those buildings were not ours," Rev. Albert Cleage, a militant member of the Central United Church of Christ, declared defiantly. "To burn down a slum-owner's shack means *he's out*. He won't come here to exploit us again."

"The criminals who committed these acts of violence against the people," said President Johnson, "deserve to be punished—and they must be punished. . . . But let us remember that it is the law-abiding Negro families who have really suffered the most at the hands of the rioters. . . . Who is really the loser when violence comes? Whose neighborhood is made a shambles? Whose life is threatened most?"

Gov. Spiro Agnew of Maryland insisted that the riots of 1967 were caused by "conspirators," but an FBI investigation found no evidence to support this charge.

"Our nation is moving toward two societies, one black, one white—separate and unequal," warned the Kerner Report. "Reaction to last summer's disorders has quickened the movement and deepened the division. . . . What white Americans have never fully understood—but what the Negro can never forget—is that white society is deeply implicated in the ghetto. White institutions created it, white institutions maintain it, and white society condones it . . . . It is time to make good the promises of American democracy to all citizens."

But Congress was so angered by the ghetto riots that it voted down the president's extended civil rights program.

The assassination of Martin Luther King in Memphis in April 1968 led infuriated mobs to riot in the ghettos of 125 cities in 29 states. "Police control problems exceeded anything ever before experienced," noted Ramsey Clark. "Traffic stopped, stores closed, windows were smashed, there was looting, arson and finally deadly violence—all to honor the fallen prophet of nonviolence. In recurring waves for several days, as if we had been seized by a nationwide fever, there was more rioting, looting and arson."

But this time the nation's police forces had begun to learn how to handle mobs properly, largely avoiding the risk of both overreaction that provoked new and higher levels of violence and inadequate action that permitted small disturbances to escalate quickly into full-scale riots.

That turbulent summer, bands of white vigilantes patrolled many cities nightly, armed with shotguns. They announced their purpose as protecting shops from looters and whites from being attacked on the streets after dark. And in the fall most American whites expressed their resentment by voting overwhelmingly for Richard M. Nixon, the presidential candidate who promised to take a tough line on law and order.

But the ghetto riots subsided principally because the majority of American blacks, who suffered most from the violence, wanted ghetto hotheads to "cool it." Many were tired of being held responsible for the violent actions of a minority. And the riots had only made things worse for black America by stiffening white opposition to ghetto grievances.

As black political leaders began to gain influence in the big cities abandoned by whites fleeing to the suburbs, there was a growing feeling in black America that maybe, after all, more was to be gained by working within the system for the needed changes than by burning it down.

15

Violence On
and Off Campus

THROUGHOUT THE 1960s and into the early 1970s college
students waged demonstrations against the Vietnam War,
police brutality, university authoritarianism, injustice to
minorities, and pollution of the environment. Most demonstrations were peaceful, except where police, troops, or
antagonists tried to break them up violently.

A small minority of students, rejecting peaceful protest as
a way to bring about reforms in the system, advocated violence as the only effective way to stop injustices. Some
formed small violent mobs for "action." Others attempted
to stampede nonviolent demonstrations into riots by provoking police attacks. The goals of this small minority were
not reform but revolution.

Most student demonstrations that broke the law usually
did so as a planned act of civil disobedience, in the spirit of
Thoreau. They staged sit-ins in university buildings, a form
of sit-down strike like those waged by CIO auto workers in
the thirties who seized auto plants to shut down production.
Their purpose was to disrupt university operations and also
the processes of the draft, but usually they attacked only
property, not persons. Hostile police, on the other hand,
often beat up the students while arresting them.

Provoked by student taunts, and sometimes by hurled objects, the police frequently ran amuck, clubbing and kicking everyone in sight, including orderly demonstrators, innocent bystanders, reporters, and cameramen. This over-reaction against unarmed demonstrators and witnesses often upset the public when it was shown on TV news programs.

The student protest movement began with the organization of the Students for a Democratic Society (SDS) in 1962, to struggle against injustices they saw in the system. Their first test of strength came in 1964 when they launched a Free Speech Movement in protest against an attempt by the University of California at Berkeley to stop students from distributing radical political leaflets.

Mario Savio, a graduate philosophy student, led SDS sit-ins at Sproul Hall, the administration building. "There is a time," he told the demonstrators, "when the operation of the machine becomes so odious, makes you so sick at heart that . . . you've got to put your bodies upon the levers . . . to make it stop. And you've got to indicate to the people who run it . . . that unless you're free, the machine will be prevented from working at all."

When university authorities called in police to remove eight hundred sit-downers, the students went limp as they were arrested and dragged off, none too gently, to detention centers. Most of the faculty grew so indignant at the spectacle of police roughing up students that they supported SDS in a student strike that shut down the university for a week.

As more and more of the students joined in anti-Establishment demonstrations, many were radicalized by police brutality. A number of police saw the students as spoiled, ungrateful scions of the middle class attacking the very system that was giving them opportunities for a university education, opportunities that few police ever had. Many students saw the police as a uniformed mob of brutal servants of the Establishment, who enjoyed beating up young people.

At Texas Southern University a student poll early in 1967 showed that 90 percent considered the Houston Police Department fair and nonviolent. However, when demonstrations brought police on campus soon afterward, students were routed violently from dormitories at gunpoint, while the police smashed their property vindictively. A new poll showed that 90 percent of the students had reversed their opinion, now regarding the Houston police as brutal and unfair.

In 1967 anti-Vietnam protests grew bigger and more strident, climaxed in October during "Stop-the-Draft Week" by a protest march on the Pentagon. For most of the day some one hundred thousand marchers staged a peaceful antiwar demonstration through Washington, but in the evening a small group of militants sought to enter the Pentagon. Soldiers and federal marshals beat many of them severely with rifle butts and batons.

"Protesters are human beings like the rest of us," warned Ramsey Clark, "and however obnoxious they may seem to many, law enforcement must not deliberately injure them. When it does, it has violated the very principle that law relies on for the order which the rioters seem to threaten."

At San Jose State College in November, police beat up students who tried to prevent campus recruiting for Dow Chemical Company, which made napalm bombs used in Vietnam.

One of the most serious police riots took place in April when SDS led student antiwar demonstrations against Columbia University for accepting grants from the Defense Department for military research. For violating a ban on indoor demonstrations, President Grayson Kirk put six SDS leaders on probation. SDS responded by seizing five university buildings for sit-in demonstrations of protest. Raising a battle cry of "Student Power!" they insisted upon a re-structure of the university to give students a voice in shaping its policies.

Kirk called in the police, who arrived on campus two hours after midnight. Breaking into the barricaded build-ings, they raced through halls and rooms with nightsticks flailing. Battered youths were punched, kicked downstairs, clubbed through a gauntlet of plainclothesmen, then hand-cuffed and arrested. In the bloody confusion, 132 students, 4 faculty members, and 12 police were injured, and 707 persons were placed under arrest.

The violent raid shocked thousands of students and faculty members, who now angrily joined a strike to shut down the university. Further battles with police caused more injuries and another 177 arrests. Now students were replying to police violence with counterviolence.

"The result of the police intervention was to create an atmosphere of violence, contempt, and hatred," reported Ellen Kay Trimberger in her book, *Campus Power Strug-gle*. "It was during the second police action that students for the first time became violent—throwing bricks at the police, smashing windows, and perhaps starting fires in several buildings. Apolitical, nonviolent students were enraged at seeing policemen beat their friends, many of whom were only spectators."

In August Kirk was compelled to resign as president of the university. Subsequently changes were made in Columbia's administration to give students a voice in policy-making.

Student alienation from the Establishment became endemic in 1968 with the Democratic National Convention in Chicago. As described in the first chapter, mobs of ram-paging police severely injured student demonstrators, reporters, and innocent bystanders, in what the Walker

Report bluntly branded "a police riot." Ramsey Clark noted, "Hundreds of thousand of young people . . . have seen a raw demonstration of police capability for violence, and they will never forget it."

In 1969, as the Vietnam War continued, millions of American students subject to the draft resisted angrily with antiwar demonstrations and sit-in protests.

At Duke University demonstrators voluntarily gave up a building they had occupied for several days, but policemen nevertheless charged into them with swinging nightsticks.

At Harvard radical students who seized an administration building and ousted nine deans were routed in a dawn raid. *The New York Times* reported that as they fled, "they were beaten and kicked by the policemen, many of whom had removed their badges [to prevent indentification]. There was no excuse for the savage club-swinging that marred the police activity." A thousand student moderates angrily joined the Harvard radicals in a three-day protest strike against the university for having called the police on campus against students.

The summer of 1969 saw a split in the student movement when radicals broke away from the SDS over the issue of violence. The rump group formed the Weathermen, a small revolutionary band that went underground to fight the Establishment with guerrilla tactics. In October they sponsored a "Four Day Rage" in Chicago, during which a mob of four hundred youths wearing crash helmets and carrying long nightsticks rampaged through the streets breaking windshields and store windows. Three were wounded by police gunfire, and 150 were arrested.

The Nixon administration saw little distinction between the violence of the Four Day Rage or subsequent dynamitings attributed to the Weathermen, and peaceful protest demonstrations. In the fall of 1969, when three hundred thousand dissenters marched on Washington, D.C., in a nonviolent Mobilization for Peace, Attorney General John Mitchell watched them from a window of his office.

"It looks like the Russian Revolution," he told his wife.

By the end of the sixties student turbulence had achieved some demands of youth. Most university administrators were listening and responding to demands for change. Many scrapped ROTC programs and Defense Department research grants and began recruiting more minority students. Student representatives were added to faculty committees and were even allowed to sit on some university governing boards.

The year 1970 continued to see campus turmoil. Trouble broke out in February between students and police at the University of California in Santa Barbara, when police arrested two student leaders at the Isla Vista area where students rented flats. A defiant mob of several hundred students rescued the prisoners, burned the squad car, and drove the police off with rocks. The mob then wrecked real estate offices that were blamed for charging exorbitant rents, and firebombed the local Bank of America as an Establishment symbol.

Proclaiming a "state of extreme emergency," Gov. Ronald Reagan imposed curfew regulations on Santa Barbara and sent in the National Guard along with police helicopters spraying tear gas. In the fighting 136 people were arrested, and a third of the county sheriff's deputies received injuries.

Peace returned to Santa Barbara only until April, when university authorities refused to let Jerry Rubin, one of the defendants in the Chicago Seven trial, speak on campus. New protest demonstrations erupted. Police brought in to break them up fired large quantities of tear gas into the crowds and wounded four students by shotgun blasts. Next day a small mob of students began setting fires, which were put out by other students, one of whom was killed by a police bullet.

"If it takes a blood bath," declared Governor Reagan, "let's get it over with. No more appeasement."

At the other extreme some students formed the Isla Vista Liberation Front to wage street battles against police and troops. One student pointed out that most members of the IVLF were subject to being drafted for Vietnam.

"A lot of them feel they only have five years to live, anyway," he said, "and they believe that, if you have any moral courage at all, the only thing left to do is fight."

In May 1970 Vice-President Spiro Agnew, who later resigned after indictment and conviction for tax fraud, accused the TV networks of encouraging student demonstrations by TV coverage and by presenting "biased news."

Federal Communications Commissioner Nicholas Johnson labeled Agnew's charges absurd. Accusing the TV networks of knuckling under to the government's demands that news coverage of protest demonstrations be stifled, Johnson warned that this censorship would "leave only the avenues of violence and despair." He criticized the networks sharply for failing to provide live coverage of the huge Mobilization for Peace in Washington to protest Nixon's expansion of the war into Cambodia.

"When the administration and big television band together," Johnson pointed out, "to suppress legitimate dissent in this country . . . when they give the president access to television tonight because he asks for it, and refuse it to the citizenry unless they demonstrate for it—it is they who are the handmaidens of revolution."

But the majority of Americans continued to regard peaceful demonstrators as the troublemakers responsible for riots. After the murder of the four uninvolved students at Kent State by national guardsmen, a Gallup poll asked the public whom they considered responsible. Of those polled, 58 percent replied, "Demonstrating students."

A lengthy investigation by a presidential commission on campus unrest, however, found the opposite to be true. And the commission warned, "The Kent tragedy must surely mark the last time that loaded rifles are issued as a matter of course to guardsmen confronting student demonstrators." Despite the refusal of an Ohio grand jury to face the truth about the murder of the students, in 1974 a federal grand jury finally indicted over half a dozen guardsmen for the Kent shootings.

With the withdrawal of American combat forces from Vietnam, the era of violent confrontations between students and the Establishment's law forces seemed to come to an end. Riot-torn campuses and cities grew peaceful.

But few observers of the American scene were willing to predict that the United States, with its long and bloody history of mob violence, had seen the last of it.

16

How Should Mobs
Be Handled?

MOST AMERICANS ARE firm supporters of law and order, but
there are millions who feel that intolerable conditions justify defiance of the law by violent behavior. Leaders of
mobs of rioting poor and underprivileged Americans have
often cited our own Revolution as their model for encouraging the oppressed to revolt against injustice.

Mobs of vigilantes who oppose disturbances of the peace
by taking the law into their own hands insist that they are
only helping to enforce law and order. Police or troops who
use unnecessary, often illegal, force against both rioting
mobs and peaceful demonstrators insist they are only doing
their duty to keep the peace.

The aggressiveness and independence that led rugged
pioneers to open and settle the Old West seems to have
taken the form of lawlessness among a number of modern-
day Americans.

"We robbed and betrayed and murdered the Indians,"
observes Dr. Benjamin Spock, noted opponent of the
Vietnam War. "We've continually abused and humiliated
black people, occasionally lynched them, murdered them,
and bombed their churches. In some frontier regions the

individual relied on his own pistols, and vigilantes dispensed justice; our fascination with this half-lawless pattern has persisted right up to the present."

In the Report of the National Commission on the Causes and Prevention of Violence (NCCPV), historian Richard M. Brown observed, "We have resorted so often to violence that we have long since become a 'trigger happy' people. . . . We must realize that violence has not been the action only of the roughnecks and racists among us but has been the tactic of the most upright and respected of our people. Having gained this self-knowledge, the next problem becomes the ridding of violence, once and for all, from the real (but unacknowledged) American value system."

One necessary step in this direction, some authorities believe, is a reduction of films and TV shows that glorify violence in Western-style shoot-outs, and gun battles waged by police, private eye, and spy heroes, suggesting to young Americans that violence is a solution to problems.

After a mob has rioted, authorities and taxpayers are often eager to uncover a "conspiracy" that caused it. If scapegoats can be found, then blame can be fastened on only a few villains and none of us need feel guilty about permitting intolerable conditions that caused the riot. And we escape unpleasant pressure to change those conditions.

This, in essence, is what happened when the urban race riots of the sixties broke out. Instead of setting up hearings to investigate and air the basic causes of those riots, Congress was stampeded into passing the 1968 Anti-Riot Act to punish the "outside agitator" who crossed state lines to "stir up trouble" and "cause riots."

But holding down the lid on a boiling pot only delays the explosion and makes it more terrible when it comes. Reason would suggest taking off the lid, letting all the scalding steam escape, and correcting the excessive temperature that caused the pot to boil over in the first place.

The spark of most ghetto riots is a real or rumored act of police brutality toward blacks. Police violence was also the spark that turned some antiwar demonstrations into riots.

Part of the problem in the sixties and early seventies was the prejudice of police against both blacks and antiwar demonstrators. The President's Commission on Law Enforcement and Administration of Justice found that of policemen working in black ghettos, 45 percent were "extremely anti-Negro," while another 34 percent admitted to prejudice.

The police were also generally conservative and offended by the dress, attitudes, and speech of young dissenters. In 1970 the Civilian Review Board of the New York City Police Department issued a report criticizing the police for using unnecessary force against students in the Columbia strike. Police officials were also taken to task for merely looking on as policemen charged students, kicking and beating them.

Critics of the police protested the shooting down of looters in ghetto riots, observing that we were the only civilized nation in the world that executed robbers instead of just arresting them. Such violence only intensified the riots, especially when the looters killed were boys as young as twelve. Ramsey Clark pointed out wryly that while looters killed no one, drunken drivers killed twenty-five thousand Americans every year, yet no one called for the instant execution of drunken drivers who were apprehended at the scene of their manslaughter.

Many Americans, content with their own status quo, tend to be unsympathetic to rebellious behavior on the part of have-nots or their defenders. The haves often demand an overforceful "get tough" policy with those who disturb their serenity.

The Lemberg Center for the Study of Violence found that the two most common causes of unsuccessful handling of riots are undercontrol and overcontrol. In the first instance, police are too inactive, letting mob disorders get out of hand. In the second instance, large forces of police, state troopers, and national guardsmen are brought in too soon, making unnecessary arrests with unnecessary brutality. Overcontrol of this kind usually provokes increased violence.

Properly trained police, the center noted, made a number of careful arrests, without violence, and dispersed or contained mobs through a variety of techniques that did not employ either clubbing or shooting. The NCCPV agreed: "Both in the short and in the long run, the use of excessive force to repress group violence often has the effect of magnifying turmoil, not diminishing it."

When racial disorders hit both Detroit and Harlem in 1943, Detroit police magnified that city's troubles into a riot by employing excessive force. In contrast, the restraint of the New York City police prevented a race riot, winning praise from both black and white community leaders.

The Kerner Report noted that some ghetto riots need never have occurred because they began only as insignificant street brawls and might have ended as just that if police had not aggravated the situation by overly aggressive law enforcement actions. The report urged recruiting better-paid, better-educated, unprejudiced police to patrol ghetto areas, with specific plans for minimizing excitement at the outbreak of disorders. They should be aided by a communications system that collects reliable information; detects, reports, and neutralizes rumors; and quickly spreads the true facts to ghetto leaders and residents to cool indignation.

Police departments in many cities have, in fact, since upgraded the quality of their recruits, carefully screening out the kind of men who seek police badges in order to give vent to sadistic desires to humiliate or beat up people. A national conference of police chiefs in 1968 developed blueprints for working out clear and quick lines of communication between the police and the ghetto to prevent build-ups of racial tension. Some cities established a "Rumor Central" phone switchboard outside police headquarters, to collect, evaluate, and counter false rumors that might lead to riots.

Many police today feel that their improved competence in handling mobs goes largely unnoticed, while the one mob in a hundred that gets out of hand and becomes a riot makes headlines.

"We prevent riots all the time," said one New York policeman. "They're the ones you never hear of."

Cities with large black or Spanish-speaking populations are placing great emphasis on recruiting police from those ethnic groups. The importance of this move was tragically illustrated in November 1973 when two white New York policemen went to the aid of a seventy-two-year-old Puerto Rican woman who had suffered a heart attack on the street.

They were giving her artificial resuscitation to save her life when a quickly gathering crowd of Puerto Ricans misunderstood the situation and thought the police were assaulting her. The language barrier between spectators and police prevented an explanation, and the mob beat the police savagely.

The Kerner Report compared thirty-eight cities that had had no riots with thirty-eight that had experienced them. It was found that twenty-four of the cities that had been spared riots had a much higher percentage of black policemen.

Once a major riot is allowed to get into full swing, it is almost impossible to suppress it, and it often takes an average of five days to run its course. Joseph D. Lohman, in his book, *The Police and Minority Groups*, declares, "If an unruly crowd has gathered, it should be possible to mobilize adequate numbers of police, quickly and without delay. A *show of force* is preferable to a belated and tragic exercise of force."

Fear of arrest is an inhibiting factor only while a crowd is uncertain, not united by a mass decision. Once the crowd turns into a mob and street battles begin raging, arrests are often then looked upon as badges of courage.

The FBI, in its study, *Prevention and Control of Mobs and Riots*, takes a dim view of the use of firearms by law enforcement agencies in handling disorders: "Under no circumstances should firearms be used until all other measures for controlling the violence have been exhausted. Above all, officers should never fire indiscriminately into a crowd or mob. Such extreme action may erupt into a prolonged and fatal clash between the officers and the mob."

The FBI also warns against the firing of weapons over the heads of a mob as a warning. "In addition to the possibility of injuring innocent persons by ricocheted bullets or poorly aimed shots, the firing may only incite the mob to further violence, through either fear or anger. At best, this is a bluffing tactic, and a basic rule when dealing with a mob is never bluff."

Maj. Gen. George Gelston, who commanded National Guard forces that quelled a race riot in Maryland in 1966, said, "I am not going to order a man killed for stealing a six-pack of beer or a television set. . . . We shot some [tear] gas out at the demonstrators and . . . in fifteen minutes there was no one in the street except the Guard. You don't have riots under those conditions. And there were no dead people . . . no kid two blocks away got hit with a stray bullet."

Under Police Commissioner Howard Leary, New York police prevented street incidents from developing into riots by quickly sending police to the scene in large numbers, so that their mere presence served to inhibit the smashing of windows, looting, and other developments that often set the stage for an escalating riot.

Some police authorities believe in sealing off riot areas rather than invading them, once a riot has begun, to give local community leaders a chance to cool it. Others believe that this policy abdicates police responsibility to maintain order and protect lives and property. What works in one riot may not always work in another. The NCCPV believes that a city's mayor and police commissioner should make this judgment between them, based on accurate facts, not rumors.

In all too many riots, highly exaggerated reports of "snipers" resulted in the tragic use of excessive force, killing and wounding large numbers of innocent people. The presence of one or two snipers in a riot should be handled by direct attempts to locate and flush them out, not by a massive armed assault on apartment buildings.

Honest mistakes by police or other law enforcement agencies need to be publicly acknowledged to earn the trust of ghetto residents. Too often, however, there is an attempt to cover up police excesses. After the 1967 Newark riot, Henry di Suvero, executive director of the New Jersey Civil Liberties Union, noted, "There is a whole conspiracy of silence, grim hostility from public officials in response to charges against the police."

"The most shocking thing," pointed out Dickinson Debevoise, head of the Newark Legal Services Project, "is that there is a tremendous outpouring of rage and determination to enforce the laws when it comes to the rioters, but no action whatsoever when the police are involved."

Albert Black, chairman of the Newark Human Rights Commission, said, "The state troopers, police, and guardsmen must admit some of the things they did here were wrong, or these people will never believe anybody again."

Similarly, when a national, state, or local government

159

employs violence against a civic disturbance, it often throws the entire blame on a few radicals or a disorderly mob. Little or nothing is said about the disorders having arisen from the enforcement of discriminatory laws, or from an unfair system that has done violence to the lives of the aggrieved minority that finally erupted in protest.

Some blame for the wild disorders of the sixties and early seventies was accepted by TV industry officials for having given live coverage to the riots, which may have had an inflammatory effect by exaggerating events or speculating about rumors. Rumors significantly aggravated tension and disorder in over 65 percent of outbreaks studied by the Kerner Report. The report also found that the greatest failure of TV in reporting the riots was a lack of informing the public of the basic reasons for the disorders—in effect, the specific grievances of those rebelling against authority.

Former Mayor John Lindsay of New York set a courageous example for other mayors in cooling off angry ghettos by walking unprotected through the crowds that gathered on Harlem's streets after the assassination of Martin Luther King, when dozens of cities were exploding with black rage.

"I put my hand on the shoulder of each man we passed," Lindsay reported, "and expressed shared sorrow. There were no words spoken in exchange, only a nod of recognition. . . . I kept moving, but finally I was hemmed in from all sides. Occasionally I could hear my name shouted, and at other times I could hear men and women weeping or moaning. . . . Several very large black men on either side of me . . . were trying to stay by my side and keep me from any possible harm."

Because New York blacks trusted Lindsay, he was able to take a firm line a few months later when a black youth was shot and killed in Bedford-Stuyvesant. A rumor spread that a white policeman had killed him without cause. A mob of blacks gathered and threatened to riot.

"I have never seen a crowd in an uglier mood," Lindsay related. ". . . I met with about eight people in the captain's room at the precinct, and for a half hour listened to pure fury. . . . I said something like: 'Look, you've got two choices. You can burn down the community or you can change it. Now, do you want to burn it down? Is that what you want to do?' "

His honest anger seemed to impress them: "They recognized that I was listening—that I was not reading from a script. . . . The very people who had made the loudest threats were subsequently instrumental in stopping rumors and helping to keep the peace."

Official terror can crush a riot, but only at a terrible cost in lives and community disillusionment with law and order. Those with great power must exercise that power carefully and justly, or stand accused of unleashing a legal violence far more deadly than the disorders they seek to quell.

This axiom is as true for college authorities as for police officials. The most peaceful campus demonstrations in the sixties and early seventies took place in those universities where the administration did not panic, negotiated with students on their demands, and showed a willingness to act on those that were reasonable. In contrast, the most violent and costly riots broke out on the campuses where authorities called in police and the National Guard.

The common feeling that united both blacks in the ghetto and students in the universities was a sense of being kept powerless, with no voice over their own lives, which had become intolerable for many reasons. These feelings reached the flash point when those in authority refused to listen to grievances, and instead sent police, guardsmen, and troops to break up protest demonstrations violently.

There are no easy, computerized answers to the problems involved in preventing crowds from turning into mobs or in dealing with riots once they occur. But most Americans agree that nonviolent solutions must be found.

Ways must be learned to allow for greater and swifter change in ending poverty, discrimination, and injustice for millions of have-not Americans. Their despair is the fuel beneath the tinder of current grievances, waiting only for new sparks to touch off new riots.

It is always too late to do anything constructive about a riot. Mass violence rarely ends without tragic consequences for many of those caught up in it, and leaves deep scars on a community that are slow to heal. Tomorrow's generation of American leaders must give priority to developing new governmental machinery that will make it unnecessary for crowds with a just grievance to degenerate into desperate mobs.

17

Mobocracy or Democracy?

THE STREETS OF the cities have become unsafe. In recent years vigilante groups have reappeared, some in support of city police, others seeking to substitute for them. Many of these groups are armed, legally or illegally.

Anthony Imperiale organized a thousand volunteers into the North Ward Citizens' Committee of Newark, providing an armed posse in support of the police. "Should a breakdown of law and order occur," he declared, "we have an arsenal."

A Jewish community in Brooklyn, beset by criminal assaults, felt inadequately protected. Some 250 volunteers organized the Maccabees to take over the functions of police vigilance in their neighborhood. Rabbi Meir Kahane, founder of the Jewish Defense League, demanded, "When every other ethnic group has rifles in their homes, why shouldn't we?"

A Scammon-Gallup survey in 1969 showed that 59 percent of blacks polled were convinced that "Negroes should arm themselves." Many ghetto vigilante groups were formed. Sometimes they demanded that police withdraw from scenes of disorder, leaving it to the vigilantes to handle mobs and prevent riots.

Police recognized some vigilante groups to the extent of issuing them special credentials to patrol their communities and cool imminent disorders. The vigilantes, however, had no legal right to use force except in self-defense and had no special powers of restraint or arrest.

Some black vigilante groups were frankly antipolice. One of the first was the Deacons for Defense and Justice, who used paramilitary forces to protect ghettos from Klan mobs in collusion with southern police. Following the Watts riot, a black Community Alert Patrol followed squad cars to maintain surveillance on police treatment of blacks.

In 1973 the New York City Police Department saw some value in utilizing citizens' groups for police work as long as they were carefully controlled. To augment thirty thousand regular police, six thousand people were uniformed as an Auxiliary Police Force, another six thousand cruised the streets in cars as a Civilian Patrol to report crimes and disorders over a citizen band network, ten thousand Block Watchers reported suspicious behavior, and there were twenty-four thousand tenant patrols of apartment houses.

The New York police frowned' on all groups who resorted to violent intervention. "There is a way to help us," said Police Sergeant John St. Jeanos, head of the volunteer program, "but it isn't by mob rule or lynch-mob psychology." In many cities where such groups insisted on their rights to operate, police have used political pressure to force them to disband.

One problem with vigilante groups is that they attract people looking for excitement, people seeking an opportunity to throw their weight around. When patrols prove boring, as most do, such people tend to go out of their way looking for trouble.

Another danger of vigilante groups is that they operate outside the law, raising the specter of paramilitary forces like Hitler's Brown Shirts and Mussolini's Black Shirts.

Does mob action accomplish its purpose when that purpose is to force change upon the Establishment? It cannot be denied that the American government was largely unresponsive to despairing cries from the ghetto until Martin Luther King's nonviolent marches were supplanted by rioters who set the cities aflame with the cry, "Burn, baby, burn!"

The Johnson and Nixon adminstrations were deaf to peaceful anti-Vietnam demonstrations until violent clashes between police, troops, and antiwar militants polarized the nation.

Urban renewal programs, and the end of the draft and withdrawal of American troops from Southeast Asia, were undoubtedly hastened by such mob-created turbulence.

Many liberals deplored violent protest, but saw it as an understandable reaction to the Establishment's stubborn refusal to heed just grievances and move in a humanitarian direction. Many radicals felt that the ends justified the means, unlike the ignoble ends of the Klan violence.

In any event, out of twenty-four race riots studied by the Kerner Commission, twenty-one led directly to the opening of communications between civil authorities and ghetto spokesmen, who began to negotiate grievances.

In many cities, however, more was lost than gained. The riots polarized racial attitudes sharply. A white backlash against blacks was expressed in attempts to cut welfare funds, impede urban renewal programs, stop integration, and apply heavier doses of "law and order" to the ghettos. Stiffer sentences were imposed on blacks in trouble with the law.

"Riots may be aimed at whites, but it is the Negroes in the ghetto who are hurt the most," also points out Algernon Black, former chairman of the New York Civilian Complaint Review Board. "It is their homes in the ghetto, their public agencies of health and hospitals and schools which

Racial tension erupted in violence in Detroit during the summer of 1967. (*Wide World Photos*)

are prevented from functioning . . . their fire department which is prevented from helping in the emergency. It is the shops and markets which supply them with food and goods and services which are burned." And even though violence might dramatize the desperation of the ghetto, it also bred counterviolence as well as the white backlash that stymied black progress.

"Nevertheless," Black concedes, "many Negroes have tended to identify with the feelings of anger and the desire to break through the feeling of powerlessness in the face of white indifference."

In 1968 it was a backlash against antiwar and ghetto turbulence that elected Richard M. Nixon president on a law-and-order-campaign. During his first term stormy demonstrations in the colleges, streets, and ghettos stiffened public opinion against accommodating protest, and Nixon was re-elected by a landslide.

Ironically, it was this administration's fear of demonstrators and critics of its policies that led to the lawless excesses, including burglary, illegal wiretapping, violations of the Constitution, setting up a secret police force, obstruction of justice, perjury, and other illegal activities exposed in the investigation of Watergate.

In the uncertain, swiftly-changing times we live in, crises of fuel, food, inflation, pollution, and unemployment follow on the heels of one another. It would be unrealistic to expect that we have seen the last of frustrations that produce demonstrations, mobs, violence, and counterviolence.

What can young Americans entering society today do to oppose and reduce the mob spirit that has wreaked such havoc on our nation and our people from the beginning?

They can recognize, first of all, that of all organizations to belong to, a mob is the worst. "The mob," said Emerson, "is man voluntarily descending to the nature of the beast." The ancient Latin moralist Seneca warned, "It is proof of a bad cause when it is applauded by a mob."

The best antitoxin one can have against mob fever is self-training in individuality, beginning with the school years. This doesn't mean becoming antisocial. But it does mean resisting pressures by one's peers to become part of any kind of a mob, or to participate in any kind of a riot.

It is not uncommon to read about mob violence at sports events, where spectators who are passionate partisans mob each other or attack referees or players who displease them. In 1973 when black and white mobs of high school students fought each other at basketball games in upstate New York, interscholastic games had to be called off because they were arousing dangerous racial tension throughout the region.

Students are less likely to become rioters when they regard themselves not as members of a mindless mob of "fans," but as unique individuals whose self-respect would be damaged by participating in a violent mass tantrum.

Teachers who encourage students to think for themselves, and to stand out against the majority whenever they believe the majority wrong, help to train young adults who strengthen democracy against mobocracy.

The thoughtful student is less susceptible to the dangerous poisons of prejudice against any race, creed, or color. Immunization is helped by learning to see groups of people not just as a faceless mass, but as collections of variegated personalities, just like ourselves and our friends.

To take violent action against any group is to deny its members the same unique identities. When we get to know someone we initially disliked because of his or her group identity, we are often surprised to discover how decent that person really is. It makes sense to judge people for themselves alone, not from any group they spring from or associate with.

One's own prejudices, often implanted by parents or a community in which one has grown up, are not a valid excuse for persisting in hostile feelings toward any minority. They should, instead, act as a challenge to one's own better nature.

It is important to distinguish between becoming part of a rioting mob and participating in a protest demonstration. The mob appeals to the basest emotions of hate and violence, temporarily uniting people in mindless savagery, running amuck, looting, arson.

A nonviolent protest demonstration, in contrast, is a cooperative expression of grievances by thinking individuals who recognize injustice, seek to correct it, and offer an intelligent program for doing so. The rioting mob is illegal.

The peaceful demonstration is a legitimate exercise of one's constitutional rights that furthers just government.

Those who join violent mobs, moreover, are far more likely to suffer injury. Even when only tear gas is used to disperse them, many may be hurt by being bowled over, trampled on, or struck by frantic rioters seeking to flee. "The escape behavior of a panic," points out the FBI, "often ruthlessly disregards the welfare of others . . . each individual taking a 'me first' attitude."

There is also always the danger of injury by police. As Yippie Abby Hoffman noted wryly, "Getting your skull cracked by a cop achieves *nothing!*"

Demonstrations motivated by love of one's fellow man are usually far more successful than those dedicated to hating him. When the Hippies went on an anti-Vietnam march in Washington, they threw nothing at the police but simply smiled and waved at them. Faced by troops with armed rifles, they merely placed flowers in the soldiers' gun barrels.

Peaceful demonstrations today are much safer for Americans than they were in the wild days of the 1968 Democratic National Convention. Bitter criticism of the police riot in Chicago has since made most police departments careful about police behavior toward nonviolent demonstrators, especially those observed by reporters for the press and TV media.

We help avoid future riots when we put pressure on our elected officials to take decisive action on community injustices that have been called to their attention. Too often officials who are quick to negotiate with minority leaders after a riot, discussing proposals and plans for reform, forget about them once the excitement ebbs away.

One eminent black leader, Dr. Kenneth B. Clark,

pointed out to the Kerner Commission that its 1968 recommendations for avoiding future ghetto riots were essentially
the same as those made by other investigating commissions
following the Chicago riot of 1919, the Harlem riot of 1935,
the Harlem riot of 1943, and the Watts riot of 1965. All
recommendations had been followed by "the same
inaction."

The Kerner Commission acknowledged that the federal
government had, indeed, been guilty of failing to follow up
on promised reforms. Warning, "It is time now to end the
destruction and the violence, not only in the streets of the
ghetto but in the lives of people," the Kerner Report called
for massive efforts to improve the status of minorities in
jobs, housing, and education, and to end once and for all
the crimes of segregation and discrimination.

Lip service was paid to those aims but little or nothing
has been done to implement them.

Black Americans, as well as all minorities, resent having
attention paid to their grievances only when trouble breaks
out, reinforcing the white majority's image of them as a vio-
lence-prone people. Throughout our history the majority
has invariably hung a "violent" tag on ethnic minorities
when they struggled for their rights—the Indians, the
French, the Irish, the Germans, the Italians, the Spanish,
the Mexicans, the Chinese, and others.

Sociologists Stanley Lieberson and Arnold J. Silverman
found in their study of race riots that "The more direct the
relation between voter and government, the less likely are
riots to occur . . . because it provides regular institutional
channels for expressing grievances."

Ghetto riots will end when the miserable conditions, the
bad schools, the dilapidated housing, the severe unemployment, and—best of all—the ghettos themselves end. Until
that time, more and more control over their own

communities, and their own lives, must be given to those forced to live there.

Most basic of all, more of us need to work at getting violence and the potential for it out of the American system.

We need to write letters to the press, local TV stations, TV networks, and theater managers to discourage glorification of violence on the nation's TV sets and film screens.

We need to put pressure on our local officials to see to it that the police department recruits only intelligent and humane officers, and that a program is instituted to teach them how to contain disorders with a minimum of force.

We need to participate in civic programs to better relations between the majority and all ethnic minorities, a program in which the police should play an important role.

It will be up to new generations of young Americans to reject the unhappy traditions of violence that have so long plagued our nation, and establish a new and more prideful tradition of nonviolence, at home and abroad.

We can all help to bring this about, not as a mob, but as a nation of persons united by that dream and determined to make it come true together, as well as one individual at a time, each in the best way we know how.

Bibliography and Recommended Reading

Acheson, Patricia C. *The Supreme Court*. New York: Dodd, Mead & Co., 1961.

Adler, Bill, ed. *Washington: A Reader*. New York: Meredith Press, 1967.

Adler, Renata. *Toward A Radical Middle*. New York: Random House, 1969.

Adler, Ruth, ed. *The Working Press*. New York: G. P. Putnam's Sons, 1966.

Allen, Frederick Lewis. *Only Yesterday*. New York: Bantam Books, 1946.

Alsop, Stewart. *The Center*. New York, Evanston, London: Harper & Row, Publishers, 1968.

*Archer, Jules. *Angry Abolitionist: William Lloyd Garrison*. New York: Julian Messner, 1969.

*———. *The Extremists*. New York: Hawthorn Books, Inc., Publishers, 1969.

*———. *Fighting Journalist: Horace Greeley*. New York: Julian Messner, 1966.

*———. *Hawks, Doves and the Eagle*. New York: Hawthorn Books, Inc., Publishers, 1970.

*———. *Mexico and the United States*. New York: Hawthorn Books, Inc., Publishers, 1973.

*———. *1968: Year of Crisis*. New York: Julian Messner, 1971.

*———. *The Plot to Seize the White House*. New York: Hawthorn Books, Inc., Publishers, 1973.

(* *indicates recommended reading*)

*————. *Resistance*. Philadelphia: Macrae Smith Company, 1973.

*————. *Revolution In Our Time*. New York: Julian Messner, 1971.

*————. *Strikes, Bombs and Bullets*. New York: Julian Messner, 1972.

*————. *They Made A Revolution: 1776*. New York, Toronto, London, Auckland, Sydney, Tokyo: Scholastic Book Services, 1973.

*————. *Treason In America*. New York: Hawthorn Books, Inc., Publishers, 1971.

*————. *The Unpopular Ones*. New York: Crowell-Collier, 1968.

Baker, Leonard. *The Johnson Eclipse*. New York: The Macmillan Co., 1966.

*Becker, Howard S., ed. *Campus Power Struggle*. Chicago: Aldine Publishing Co., 1970.

*Black, Algernon D. *The People and the Police*. New York, Toronto, London, Sydney: McGraw-Hill, 1968.

*Block, Irvin. *Violence in America*. New York: Public Affairs Committee, Inc., 1970.

Blumberg, Abraham S., ed. *The Scales of Justice*. Chicago: Aldine Publishing Co., 1970.

Broudy, Eric; Halliburton, Warren; and Swinburne, Laurence. *They Had A Dream*. New York: Pyramid Books, 1969.

Chapin, Bradley. *Provincial America*. New York: The Free Press, 1966.

*Chaplin, J. P. *Rumor, Fear and the Madness of Crowds*. New York: Ballantine Books, 1959.

Chute, William J. *The American Scene: 1600–1860*. New York, Toronto, London: Bantam Books, 1964.

————. *The American Scene: 1860 to the Present*. New York, Toronto, London: Bantam Books, 1966.

*Clark, Ramsey. *Crime In America*. New York: Simon and Schuster, 1970.

*Cleaver, Eldridge. *Post-Prison Writings and Speeches*. New York: Random House, 1969.

*Commager, Henry Steele. *Freedom and Order*. Cleveland and New York: The World Publishing Co., 1968.

*Committee on Un-American Activities. *Guerrilla Warfare Advocates in the United States*. Washington, D.C.: U.S. Government Printing Office, 1968.

*Conant, Ralph W. *The Prospects For Revolution*. New York, Evanston, London: Harper & Row, Publishers, 1971.

Currey, Cecil B. *Road to Revolution*. Garden City, New York: Doubleday & Co., 1968.

*Dorson, Richard M., ed. *American Rebels*. New York: Pantheon, 1953.

Bibliography and Recommended Reading

Eisenhower, Dwight D. *Mandate For Change*. Garden City, New York: Doubleday & Co., 1963.

——. *Waging Peace*. Garden City, New York: Doubleday & Co., 1965.

*Epstein, Jason. *The Great Conspiracy Trial*. New York: Random House, 1970.

*Graham, Hugh Davis, and Gurr, Ted Robert. *The History of Violence In America*. New York, Toronto, London: Bantam Books, 1969.

*Grant, Joanne. *Black Protest*. Greenwich, Connecticut: Fawcett Publications, 1968.

*Grimshaw, Allen D. *Racial Violence in the United States*. Chicago: Aldine Publishing Co., 1969.

Gunther, John. *Inside U.S.A.* New York and London: Harper & Brothers, 1947.

*Headley, Joel Tyler. *The Great Riots of New York: 1712 to 1873*. New York: The New American Library, 1965.

Heffner, Richard D. *A Documentary History of the United States*. New York: The New American Library, 1965.

*——, and Wallace, Michael, eds. *American Violence*. New York: Vintage Books, 1971.

Hofstadter, Richard, ed. *Great Issues in American History*. New York: Vintage Books, 1958, 1969.

Holbrook, Stewart T. *Dreamers of the American Dream*. Garden City, New York: Doubleday & Co., 1957.

*Jensen, Joan M. *The Price of Vigilance*. Chicago, New York, San Francisco: Rand McNally & Co., 1968.

Johnson, Lyndon B. *The Vantage Point*. New York: Popular Library, 1971.

Krock, Arthur. *In The Nation: 1932-1966*. New York, Toronto, London, Sydney: McGraw-Hill, 1966.

Lasch, Christopher. *The New Radicalism In America*. New York: Vintage Books, 1967.

*Leinwand, Gerald, ed. *Civil Rights and Civil Liberties*. New York: Washington Square Press, 1968.

Lens, Sydney. *Poverty Yesterday and Today*. New York: Thomas Y. Crowell Co., 1973.

Leuchtenburg, William E. *Franklin D. Roosevelt and the New Deal*. New York: Harper & Row, Publishers, 1963.

Lindsay, John V. *The City*. New York: W. M. Norton & Co., Inc., 1969.

Lippmann, Walter. *Early Writings*. New York: Liveright, 1970.

*Lukas, J. Anthony. *The Barnyard Epithet and Other Obscenities.* New York, Evanston, London: Harper & Row, Publishers, 1970.

*————. *Don't Shoot—We Are Your Children!* New York: Dell Publishing Co., 1972.

Marden, Charles F. *Minorities in American Society.* New York, Cincinnati, Chicago, Boston, Atlanta, Dallas, San Francisco: American Book Co., 1952.

*Markmann, Charles Lam. *The Noblest Cry.* New York: St. Martin's Press, 1965.

*Marx, Gary T., and Archer, Dane. "Citizen Involvement in the Law Enforcement Process: The Case of Community Police Patrols." Paper presented to Annual Meeting of American Political Science Association, Los Angeles, 1970.

Matthews, Herbert L. *A World In Revolution.* New York: Charles Scribner's Sons, 1971.

McCord, John H., ed. *With All Deliberate Speed: Civil Rights Theory and Reality.* Urbana, Chicago, London: University of Illinois Press, 1969.

Merrill, Walter M. *Against Wind and Tide.* Cambridge, Massachusetts: Harvard University Press, 1963.

Miles, Michael W. *The Radical Probe.* New York: Atheneum, 1971.

Miller, Douglas T. *Jacksonian Aristocracy.* New York: Oxford University Press, 1967.

**Mississippi Black Paper.* New York: Random House, 1965.

Mitau, G. Theodore. *Decade of Decision.* New York: Charles Scribner's Sons, 1967.

Mitgang, Herbert. *America at Random.* New York: Coward-McCann, 1969.

Moquin, Wayne, and Van Doren, Charles, eds. *A Documentary History of the Mexican Americans.* Toronto, New York, London: Bantam Books, 1972.

Morris, Richard B., ed. *Great Presidential Decisions.* Greenwich, Connecticut: Fawcett Publications, 1966.

*Myers, Gustavus. *History of Bigotry in the United States.* New York: Capricorn Books, 1960.

————. *History of the Great American Fortunes.* New York: The Modern Library, 1937.

*National Commission on the Causes and Prevention of Violence. *Rights In Conflict.* (Walker Report). New York: The New American Library, 1968.

175

Bibliography and Recommended Reading

*Newfield, Jack. *A Prophetic Minority*. New York: The New American Library, 1967.

Nye, Russel B. *William Lloyd Garrison and the Humanitarian Reformers*. Boston, Toronto: Little, Brown and Co., 1955.

Osborne, John. *The Second Year of the Nixon Watch*. New York: Liveright, 1971.

*Porambo, Ron. *No Cause For Indictment*. New York, Chicago, San Francisco: Holt, Rinehart and Winston, 1971.

Pringle, Henry F. *Theodore Roosevelt*. New York: Harcourt, Brace & World, 1956.

*Pullen, John J. *Patriotism in America*. New York: American Heritage Press, 1971.

*Rainwater, Lee, ed. *Soul*. Chicago: Aldine Publishing Co., 1970.

Report of the National Advisory Commission on Civil Disorders. (Kerner Report.) New York: E.P. Dutton & Co., 1968.

*Riesman, David; Glazer, Nathan; Denney, Reuel. *The Lonely Crowd*. Garden City, New York: Doubleday & Co., 1953.

Rollins, Alfred B., Jr. *Woodrow Wilson and the New America*. New York: Dell Publishing Co., 1965.

*Rubenstein, Richard E. *Rebels in Eden: Mass Political Violence in the United States*. Boston, Toronto: Little, Brown and Co., 1970.

*Sanders, Helen Fitzgerald, and Bertsche, William H., Jr., eds. *X. Beidler: Vigilante*. Norman: University of Oklahoma Press, 1957.

Sarles, Frank B., Jr., and Shedd, Charles E. *Colonials and Patriots*. Washington, D.C.: U.S. Department of the Interior, National Park Service, 1964.

Scheer, George F., and Rankin, Hugh F. *Rebels and Redcoats*. New York: The New American Library, 1959.

Segal, Ronald. *Race War*. New York: The Viking Press, 1967.

*Shannon, David A. *The Great Depression*. Englewood Cliffs, N.J.: Prentice-Hall, 1960.

Sherrill, Robert. *Gothic Politics in the Deep South*. New York: Grossman Publishers, 1968.

*Sinkler, George. *The Racial Attitudes of American Presidents*. Garden City, New York: Doubleday & Co., 1971.

Snyder, Louis L., and Morris, Richard B., eds. *They Saw It Happen*. Harrisburg, Pennsylvania: The Stackpole Co., 1951.

Spender, Stephen. *The Year of the Young Rebels*. New York: Vintage Books, 1969.

*Spock, Benjamin. *Decent and Indecent*. New York: The McCall Publishing Co., 1970.

*Starkey, Marion L. *The Devil in Massachusetts*. New York: Alfred A. Knopf, 1949.

Steffens, Lincoln. *The World of Lincoln Steffens*. New York: Hill and Wang, 1962.

*Stein, David Lewis. *Living the Revolution: The Yippies in Chicago*. Indianapolis, New York: The Bobbs-Merrill Company, 1969.

*Stone, I. F. *The Killings at Kent State*. New York: A New York Review Book, 1971.

Syrett, Harold C., ed. *American Historical Documents*. New York: Barnes & Noble, 1960.

*Thayer, George. *The Farther Shores of Politics*. New York: Simon and Schuster, 1968.

Truman, Harry S. *Year of Decisions*. New York: The New American Library, 1965.

——. *Years of Trial and Hope*. New York: The New American Library, 1965.

*Valentine, Alan. *Vigilante Justice*. New York: Reynal & Co., 1956.

Weigley, Russell F. *Towards An American Army*. New York and London: Columbia University Press, 1962.

Wheeler, Harvey. *Democracy In a Revolutionary Era*. Santa Barbara, California: The Center For the Study of Democratic Institutions, 1970.

Wills, Garry. *Nixon Agonistes*. Boston: Houghton Mifflin Co., 1970.

*——. *The Second Civil War*. New York: The New American Library, 1968.

Also consulted were issues of *The American Legion Magazine, The Center Magazine, The Harvard Bulletin, The Nation, Newsweek, The New York Herald Tribune, New York Magazine, The New York Review of Books, The New York Times, Psychology Today, The Saturday Evening Post, TV Guide, University: A Princeton Quarterly,* and *Variety.*

Index

179